P9-EKX-241

LUKE G. WILLIAMS

AMERICAN ENTREPRENEUR

Luke G. Williams

American Entrepreneur

A Memoir
by the Father of the
Electronic Sign Industry

TRADE MARK PRESS
SPOKANE, WASHINGTON 2002

Copyright 2002 by Luke G. Williams

All rights reserved

Manufactured in the United States of America

Family photos by permission of Luke G. Williams,
copyright 2002 by Luke G. Williams.

Cover and book design by Scott Poole

Library of Congress Cataloging-in-Publication Data

   Williams, Luke G.1923-

   Luke g. williams : an american entrepreneur : a memoir

   ISBN 0-9714764-0-3 (hardcover: alk paper)

     1. Williams, Luke G., 1923- 2. Businessmen--United States--Biography.

   3. American Sign & Indicator Company. I. Title.

HC102.5 W545 A3 2001

338.7'617416--dc21

[B]   200156359

I would like to thank the people who helped me with this book. I want to thank my daughter Brenda and son Mark for their encouragement and support. My dear wife Lucy helped me read and edit every chapter. My secretary of forty years, Ethel Schuerman, Lucy's son-in-law, Greg Hughes, and Kris Pederson, transcribed my dictation. I appreciate the editorial help of Bill Stimson, a professor at Eastern Washington University, and also Scott Poole, for his work on the design of the book.

Contents

Preface

As I look back over nearly eight decades of life, I am amazed to think of the rich experiences and privileges I have had. My brother Chuck and I invented the world's first alternating time-and-temperature display. Our original sign, which we bolted to the side of a Spokane bank in 1951, is recognized by the Smithsonian Institution as the forerunner of the ever-changing message sign that is familiar to nearly everyone in the world today. Based upon this invention, Chuck and I founded the American Sign and Indicator Company. It grew to become the largest electronic sign company in the world at that time.

That a person born to a poor family and blessed with just a few God-given abilities, and perhaps a few more instilled by his parents, could have developed five profitable businesses, come to befriend presidents of the United States, help stage a World's Fair, and be elected to head the National Association of Manufacturers, just amazes me. I believe I owe my success to our Founding Fathers and my luck of being born into a nation that allowed individual freedom and free enterprise.

When I completed my term as chairman of the National Association of Manufacturers (NAM), I was presented with a bronze statue depicting a weary man riding atop a weary horse. The inscription reads: "Luke Williams — Circuit Rider for the Gospel of Free Enterprise." Of all the kind honors I have received in my life, this one has a special meaning to me. I have always believed individual freedom is the mainspring of human progress, and as the statue inscription suggests, I have been willing to speak out for freedom and free enterprise.

I continue to talk about the advantages of that system here. This book is my personal testimony to what a wonderful country America is.

Luke G. Williams
Spokane, Washington

LUKE G. WILLIAMS

AMERICAN ENTREPRENEUR

1

Family

Many years later my older sister Helen described the night of my birth to me. She remembered it very vividly. A brisk wind with an early fall chill rustled through the trees and the frame dwelling at East 13200 Mission Road in Pinecroft, Washington. We did not have a telephone so my father sent Helen, who was eleven at the time, and my older brother Bill, who was nine, out into the night with a kerosene lantern to tell Doctor Rusk that Grace Williams was in labor.

It would be Grace Williams' fifth childbirth, but this was not an easy one. Another sister, Jean, told me decades later that she could still remember my mother's screams of pain. Finally the screams stopped and were followed by the cry of a baby, and I was born on October 4, 1923.

Family tradition was to name Williams children to honor previous generations. Helen was named for my mother's mother, Helen Craig Murray. My other sister was named after my mother's sister, Jean Murray Hadley. My oldest brother, Bill, was named after my mother's brother, Bill Murray. My older brother Charles was named after my mother's father, Charles

*The Williams family in Virginia. My father is standing
in the foreground between his father and mother.*

*The Williams family farm near Marion, Virginia, where
my father grew up.*

Murray. I guess by this time it was my father's turn. They named me Luke Gladstone Williams, most always shortened to Lukie.

I am sure, or at least I hope, that I took more than my name from ancestors. My father, Luke C. Williams, was one of seven children born to Noah B. Williams and Emma Cooper Williams of Tilson's Mills, Smyth County, in southwest Virginia. Grandma Williams was the daughter of a doctor in the Confederate Army. She told me that as a young girl of seven, she had a clear recollection of the Yankee Army (Sheridan's) coming through their valley. The soldiers burned their house and barn, took all of their cattle, hogs, and chickens, and left them standing in the ashes with nothing but the clothes on their backs. Grandma said the family had saved some Confederate money, hidden in an old stump, which of course turned out to be worthless.

Much of what my father told me about his early years in Tilson's Mills had to do with how hard everyone worked. The whole family helped farm the small tract of land, approximately 80 acres. Grandpa Williams also ran a tannery, and the tanning of leather was very difficult work in those days, a process of soaking and rubbing that took months. Grandpa also raised turkeys. After butchering them, he would have to drive them twelve miles over the hill to the railheading in Marion to be shipped to a city. Sometimes when Grandpa arrived in Marion the turkeys were spoiled, or the people who received them would not want to buy them, and in either case an enormous amount of work would be lost.

At that time in Virginia most people operated sawmills on their farms. Some cousins in the Williams family by the name of Hubble moved to the timber-rich hills of northern Idaho, set up a mill, and prospered. Noah and Emma Williams heard about it and decided to sell the Virginia farm and their belongings and follow their cousins to Idaho. This is quite a story in itself, and my father's sister, Foye Williams Krause, has related it in some detail in the family history.

In Idaho, Grandfather Noah farmed and later built and operated a hotel and restaurant in Bonners Ferry. Eventually he sold that hotel and bought the still-existing Collins Hotel in Spokane. He operated that hotel until his retirement. Grandpa and Grandma Williams had a big house in the Spokane Valley not far from my parents', and I remember running roughshod through it with various cousins.

My father, after arriving in Bonners Ferry with his parents, went to work in a general merchandise store as a clerk. Luke C. Williams was a handsome and personable man and a born

My grandfather, Noah Williams, in the straw hat and black coat, and grandmother, Emma, to his left, surrounded by members of the Williams family.

salesman. He had, I believe, just six years of school, but he was good with figures and wrote well. He wrote poetry all his life. I have a book of his poems that reflect the warm spirit that was the soul of Luke C. Williams. In about 1907, Dad moved down the road to Coeur d' Alene to take another job in a store. Soon after arriving he met my mother.

My mother, Grace Murray, was born on August 28, 1889, on a farm in Colbyville, Minnesota, a small town near Duluth. Two of mother's cousins, Marion Murray Burlingame and Margaret Murray Joyce, took me to the location of this farm in 1980. All the buildings were gone and the property was now covered in trees. Like the Williams, my mother's family, the Murrays, had migrated west to the hills of north Idaho. The Murrays settled farther south on Copper Creek, near Kingston, Idaho. They later moved a short distance and homesteaded on the south side of the Coeur d' Alene River, a mile south of the famous mission settlement of Cataldo, Idaho.

Since my grandfather, Charles Murray, died of cancer in 1919, before I was born, all I knew of him was his reputation as an excellent carpenter and a good father. I saw for myself the barn Grandfather built was a masterpiece of hand-hewn carpentry. It was roofed with cedar shakes he had split himself. Grandma, or "Gommie," as we called her, continued to live in the cabin with her son Bill until her death in 1932, and I have fond memories of spending some weeks each summer there with her and Bill.

I was very close to Uncle Bill, my mother's only sibling. He never married. Except for a tour of duty with the Army during World War I, he spent his entire life in the backwoods of Idaho. Uncle Bill was a real mountain man, able to live comfortably in the mountains. He was a bit eccentric, and he believed that since he served in the First World War he never needed to buy a

Uncle Bill.

*Uncle Bill, with a
couple of nieces, and
Gommie.*

license for anything ever again. To the best of my knowledge he never did. He contracted to cut timbers used to shore up the tunnels of north Idaho's mines. Chuck and I used to visit him in the 1930s and he would take us into the woods for the purpose of picking huckleberries and fishing. He was always very friendly and pleasant. He treated us as pals and not as boys. His conversation was sprinkled with the remarks, "Is that a fact," and, "I'll be damned."

I recall one time that we went to Cataldo to visit him for a two-week vacation. He was not at the cabin, and Chuck and I knew about where he was on Pine Creek. We drove up this logging road for about ten miles and came upon his camp. We got there in the afternoon, and Uncle Bill never showed up until about ten o'clock at night, when he came walking into camp, just suddenly appearing. He didn't have a shirt on, and he had been out picking huckleberries. He was very pleased to see us, and always laughed and had a big chuckle.

Uncle Bill used to tell Chuck and me about his confrontations with the law and game wardens over the fact that he did not buy licenses. He really believed that he never needed to buy a license because he had served in the Army. He laughed as he told us that when the game warden came to visit his cabin, he would serve up bear meat, and the game warden was afraid to say anything about it, though he knew Bill Murray never bought a license.

Somewhere along the line Bill Murray had purchased some stock in the Sunshine Mine for a few pennies a share. The stock went up to $25 a share in the early 1930s, and Bill sold out. He probably had only two or three hundred shares, but this amounted to a big sum of money during the Depression. To celebrate his new-found wealth, Bill took the train back to Chicago, visited the World's Fair in 1934, and went on to Detroit and bought a brand new 1934 Plymouth sedan, which he drove back to north Idaho. A license was provided on the car when he took it from the Chrysler Motor Company, but to the best of my knowledge Uncle Bill never bought another license for the car as long as he lived.

Uncle Bill did not drink and had no bad habits. In 1946 he was arrested in Wallace, Idaho for being drunk. He was kept in jail for two or three days until they were able to get hold of my mother. She and Dad went up and got Uncle Bill. It turned out that he was not drunk, but had suffered a stroke and could not walk or talk. I am sure not receiving any care or treatment during those first few days did not bode well for him. Mom and Dad took him home with them and Mom spent the next five months nursing Bill in a little house in our back yard until he died of the stroke.

It has always bothered me that I did not attend Bill's funeral. I was just married and on vacation at Hayden Lake, near Coeur d' Alene. It wasn't that I had anything but love and admiration for Uncle Bill, but I was just socially ignorant about the importance of such things. I know that my mother never forgave me, nor did I forgive myself. Bill Murray was a fine person, and Chuck and I spent many wonderful days and vacations with him in the woods in North Idaho. I have always felt very bad that I failed to perform this one important responsibility. My youthful neglect contrasts poorly with my mother's loving care for Bill during his final illness before he died.

Mother had actually been a nurse decades earlier, when she and her brother Bill were teenagers. She went through nurse's training at the military hospital in Coeur d' Alene, Idaho, and was working in the post hospital when Luke C. Williams, the store clerk recently come down from Bonners Ferry, met her. They were married on September 30, 1907.

They moved to Pinecroft, between Coeur d' Alene and Spokane, Washington, and began an unbelievably busy life holding together a family of six children through the difficulties of the first half of the twentieth century. The constant economic ups and downs of Luke and Grace Williams are reflected in the fact that each of their six children would be born in a different house. I can see this now, looking back. But I suppose I will never really appreciate my parents' struggles and sacrifices for me. All I remember about that period is that it was the most carefree and wonderful childhood any boy could want.

Me, age 2, at our house at Pinecroft in the Spokane Valley.

2

Early
Childhood

My first recollection of my life is a rather shadowy vision of my brother Chuck and me in the yard of our home in Pinecroft with a shovel and hoe. We were enterprising hole diggers at that time, and spent much of our time digging holes, hoeing the garden, and generally finding "things to do" in a rural area.

A more vivid memory of my earliest years was the time mother was driving Helen to school at Trentwood and I opened the door in the back seat. In those days, the doors opened from the front to the back, and when the door caught the wind it flew open and I flew out. We were probably going about 25 or 30 miles per hour, and I got scuffed up pretty badly and had a sizeable cut on my forehead. Mother drove me to Dr. Rusk's house and he sewed me up. No pain medications were available or needed, since the doctor said he would give me a nickel if I

Much of my childhood I spent
digging. What for I don't know.

didn't cry. I never let out a peep. I had never owned a nickel before.

Mother always had a large garden and she was a great cook. She made homemade bread, biscuits, and gravy. I distinctly remember Mother's and sister Helen's devil's food cake. I loved chocolate, and still do. It was probably chocolate that etched on my memory trips to downtown Spokane with my mother. I recall distinctly that she always stopped in at the Kress or Newberry's stores and bought chocolate. Usually it was broken chocolate or little chocolate kisses. A less pleasing memory of one of these trips is the time Mother took me to the restroom in the Palace Department Store and I flushed her purse down the toilet.

I have the clear impression that Chuck and I were into more than a little mischief. We usually got along with Mom during the day, although I remember I got my first spanking for trying to run away from her once when commanded to come. I also remember that I first learned great respect for my father when Chuck and I got into a rough pillow fight in our room. Dad licked us with a razor strap. It really wasn't very cruel punishment but it put an awesome fear into us. There were not many times in our young lives when Dad would punish us, because the few times it happened we remembered it. Dad was a loving and patient father, however, when I think back about some of the trials he was having with his business at the time. He was probably under a considerable amount of stress.

I remember one time Chuck and I walked about a half-mile from our house to the Spokane River—we were about six and four years old. There was a fellow in a boat who offered to row us across the river and we readily accepted. In the meantime, Mother had missed us and was frantically hunting for us. I suppose that the river was probably one of the first places that a mother would go, and when she got there we were just approaching the far side of the river. The fellow told Mother that he would bring us back, but she insisted that he go to the closest shore. She drove miles down to the Green Street Bridge and up the other side of the river to pick us up. We got a very good scolding, and probably a paddling, but I also remember that mother was very glad to find us. That she was not overreacting was proven by a tragedy that happened on the river about that time. A neighbor family, the Jacksons, lost four of their children when their raft caught the current and went down the river and over the dam. Four children from one family was a tragic loss.

I don't have a very good recollection of my brother Bill during this time, since he was nine years older. He was a born mechanic and wherever we lived found jobs repairing automobile and airplane engines to help the family finances. My oldest sibling, Helen, was eleven years older than I. From the time I was little she held a good job at the Crescent department store in downtown Spokane, which helped my parents financially. I recall cheerful Helen cleaning our house while listening to an old gramophone. One of her favorite songs was "She's a Pretty Little Dear." The lyrics went like this: "She's a pretty little dear and she lives uptown, her Daddy is a butcher and his name is Brown. Her beauty is of high renown, and she's the girl for me. I took the girl to a restaurant, the finest in the state. She said she wasn't hungry, but I'll tell you what she ate. Applesauce, asparagus, soft-shelled crab on toast. I thought I'd die, when she asked for pie, for I had but 50 cents." It's strange the little things that you remember.

Helen was wonderful at helping Mother with housework. Jean, four years younger, was a little less domestically inclined, but she was a great spirit and very good at attracting boyfriends. She could play the piano by ear and could play any tune that she could hum. She was also quite dramatic. One of her favorite pastimes was to play very sad songs on the piano and narrate them. Her primary goal was to get Chuck and me crying, which she did quite often. She would play these melodies and tell us about little birds that had broken wings and legs and couldn't find their mothers. It was funny to her but it was very sad to us. Tears were plentiful.

In those days neighbors seemed very important to our daily lives. The McHenrys lived next to us and under the water tower. They had three sons, Don, Delbert, and Dale ("Squeaky"). Mrs. McHenry used to make delicious homemade root beer. It was a

Four of the Williams kids. From the left, Bob, me, Chuck, Jean, and a cousin, Mary Jean.

The earliest known photo of the partners in Williams Brothers, Luke on the left and Chuck on the right.

My cousin, Mary Jean, on the left, and my sisters, Helen and Jean.

14

great treat to have her provide us with cold root beer on hot summer days. The Fisher family lived next door to us on the north. They had two daughters about the same age as Chuck and me. Chuck and I played with them a lot, and I think this was probably the first time I learned that there was a difference between boys and girls. My parents were also close to George and Clara Berg, both of them school teachers. It was their son's experiences in the submarine service a dozen years later that would make me anxious to go into the Navy.

I recall one incident during this period, which I suppose illustrates that parents of large families have little hope for peaceful lives. One fall, Chuck and I were playing at a neighbor's house. The neighbors were burning leaves and Chuck and I were having fun running through the smoldering leaves. I had a brand new pair of Levi pants on. When you got a new pair of pants at my age, they were always two sizes too large so that you could grow into them. The cuffs of my pants were rolled up and evidently I captured a spark inside one cuff. Suddenly my pants leg blazed up in fire. I remember that a teenage neighbor, one of the Blegen boys, saw what happened and rolled me on the ground and smothered the fire. It was rather frightening for my folks, but there was no real damage done to me other than some minor burns on my legs.

I was enrolled in the Orchard Center Elementary School. My very first recollection of school is of standing in the classroom at the school, very close to my mother's skirts, being introduced to the teacher and being reassured by my mother. This was September of 1929 and I was not quite six years old. When my mother left I was a very lonely little boy very much in awe of and suspicious of my new surroundings and circumstances.

Chuck was just enough older that he went to another school. It was the first time in my life I experienced being without him.

Orchard Center Elementary School is still located at the corner of Park and Buckeye in the Spokane Valley, though it has been expanded considerably since then. I remember a building of just two classrooms, with 20 children in each of the first and second grades. We learned to read by the phonics method, to write by the Palmer method, and to answer questions. We used the blackboard, pencil and paper, and of course, crayons. We learned the disciplines of a classroom that involved timeliness, recess, play, and fire drills.

During these years Dad was owner of the largest sign company in Spokane. His shop was in the 100 block on West Riverside, Spokane's main drag. He painted signs and pictures, and also made the new electric signs. These signs had light bulbs on the painted letters to light them and along the edges to attract attention. He later even animated these signs.

Though hard at work trying to make a go of the sign business all of his life, my father really had the heart of an artist. He loved painting his murals of western vistas and he wrote poetry for relaxation. Here are some samples of his poems:

from *Winter*

Oh, winter, how beautiful thy snow
    That comes like angels in flight
From out of the heavens to the earth below,
    So gentle, so pretty and white.
To give us a change in color scheme,
    To cover with a blanket white
The hills, the mountains, the valleys green
    And the song birds put to flight.
The flower beds have shed their bloom,

The cherry tree is bare,
The weeping willow hangs in gloom,
Its head in cold despair. . . .

from *There's a Little House Across the Valley*

For in that little house across the valley
      The angels came one night
And took my mother up to heaven
      Tho' I never thought it right.
The angels must have loved her
      And the song she used to sing,
While she held me close to her bosom,
      Oh, dear angels, won't you bring
My mother back to me
      And let her sing again
That lullaby she used to sing. . . .

from *To My Wife*

I plucked you in prime
      From out of field of maidens sublime,
You are the flower
      That bloomed in my heart,
Dearer and sweeter
      Than the pretty love dart.
And from the stem of your body
      Came six little flowers,
To freshen with smiles
      Like balmy May showers.
They're vigorous and growing,
      And soon they will bloom,
Their sweetness and fragrance
      Will incense the gloom.
Their resemblance bear witness

To the sweetness of you,
To the bright shining sun
That gathers the dew.
And when thy petals have fallen
And thy stems lie dead,
More flowers will be blooming
From the seed that thou shed.
But none shall be grander
Or sweeter than you,
That added six little blossoms
To sweeten the dew
That falls with the darkness
And leaves with the light,
Oh, mother, sweet mother,
God's flower of light.

These poems capture a tenderness that I remember in my father.

I was six when the stock market crashed in 1929 and that's about when Dad's business problems began. The fall-off in business because of the Depression was compounded by problems in Dad's other business interest. Dad had a love and a compulsion for mine speculation. He dreamed of making a fortune when the next shot of powder uncovered the "mother lode." In the 1920s he was grubstaking miners, giving them tools, food, and some money, so they could go off into the mountains and prospect. It is probable that Dad, a naturally generous man, did it partially out of the goodness of his heart, but I'm sure he always figured he would make his fortune when one of these miners struck rich ore.

Dad grubstaked one individual who prospected in the area just west and south of Thompson Falls, Montana. This individual came back to town and had ore samples which were of quite high grade. This excited Dad considerably. The man had staked the claim as the "Lucky Luke Mining Company" since Dad had put up the grubstake. Dad got several people in the Spokane Valley interested in developing the mine and a company was formed. Sidney Smith took over the presidency of the mine, and they developed it to a degree, but nothing ever came from it. The investors, including my father, lost all their money.

Dad never gave up hope that there was fabulous wealth in the "Lucky Luke Claim" and talked about it for years. Thirty years later, Chuck and I employed two geologists from the American Mining and Smelting Company to go to Clark Fork and examine the property. The geologists spent two or three days on the property and reported that there were probably not any commercial quantities of ore on this claim. Chuck Williams had Ed Muster do some work on the claims for a number of years, but the dream of Luke C. Williams and the Lucky Luke Mine in Thompson Falls faded into emptiness.

Dad later became interested in the Crystal City Mine in Miles, Washington, at the confluence of the Spokane and Columbia Rivers. A geologist had assured him, "Luke, you and I might not live to see it, but there is going to be a great mine there someday." Through the 1920s Dad invested and lost a good deal of money in this mine as well. About 1955, Chuck and I formed another company, the Crystal City Mining Company, and raised some money to have the water pumped out of the mine so geologists could examine it. They determined there were places you could chip out rock that had a high level of lead and silver and zinc, but not in large enough quantities to be commercially profitable. The mine also had tungsten and our brother Bob Williams worked for a long time down there blasting and digging out some of these deposits. But it turned out there were no commercial amounts of tungsten either. The Crystal City Mine was sold in 1985 for $50,000 to a geologist.

The proceeds of the sale had to be distributed to some 70 shareholders. I don't know why the geologist bought the mine, but it would be wonderful to learn one day that Dad's dream came true.

During the time of his interest in these mines, Dad had neglected the sign business. He had actually set up a mining office in the Symon Building in downtown Spokane, furniture and all. I am not sure, but I suspect the mining losses were the reason Dad decided to sell his property in Spokane and close his sign business to move to an undeveloped farm in Valley, Washington, about 50 miles north of Spokane. Aside from his personal business problems, this was the onset of the Great Depression. It would be easier to feed a large family on a farm.

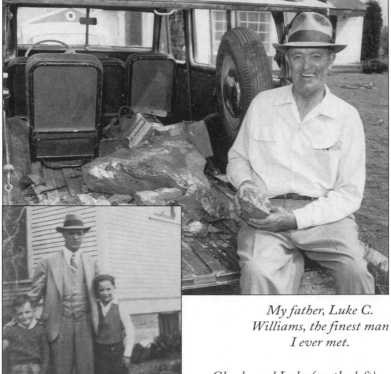

My father, Luke C.
Williams, the finest man
I ever met.

Chuck and Luke (on the left)
with Dad about 1930.

3

Move to the Ranch

Shortly after I entered the third grade, my parents traded our house in the Spokane Valley for a 160-acre ranch in Cottonwood, Washington. Cottonwood was not even a town but only a mail designation in the hilly farm country 50 miles north of Spokane, near Chewelah, Washington.

Dad, Grandpa Williams, and brother Bill built a house on the farm entirely out of a local product called Thermax, which was manufactured at the Magnesite plant near the ranch. It was an insulated product that was made from minerals from a nearby quarry. It looked like loosely-packed particle board. It was heavy and had good insulation qualities, and it was cheap.

The house was a two-story structure, about 40 feet long and probably about 30 feet wide. The first floor had a large kitchen and living room. Upstairs, Jean and Bill had small rooms. Chuck and I slept together and sometimes Bob along with us. Sister Helen stayed behind in Spokane so she could keep her well-

Luke (left) and Chuck on The Ranch.

paying job, $13.20 a week, at the Crescent department store. Helen stayed at Aunt Faye and Uncle Joe Williams' house, Dad's brother, which was a great help to Helen.

The farm consisted of 160 acres. There were between 60 and 80 acres of timber and uncleared fields. We used the 80 acres of farmland to grow hay and wheat. There was an old barn on the land about an eighth of a mile from the location my mother chose to put the house. This constituted a slight logistical problem, so we had to build a second barn closer to the house, about 100 yards to the north. Not long ago I revisited the farm and found that these buildings are no longer there. The new occupants built a new house and are in the dairy business.

Our closest neighbors, the Graves, lived about a half-mile down the road toward a little town called Valley. Beyond the Graves lived the Peternells and the Masciniks. Farther to the east, probably about a mile from our house, lived Mr. Kirchina and his son Louie. Louie was my age and we became good school buddies. To the north of us, approximately three-quarters of a mile, lived the Sears family. Alvie Sears, a World War I veteran, ran the farm and took care of elderly parents. He would become a mentor, of a sort, to Chuck and me.

The farm could feed a large family at little expense. What money we needed Dad had to earn by roving the region for sign-painting jobs. Consequently, Dad was gone much of the time during these years and I spent very little time with him. This is probably why I enjoyed any chance I got to work with Dad in the fields or on other projects.

Dad took Chuck and me on one of his trips in his 1926 touring sedan. We went to Spokane and then down to Coulee Dam, which was then just beginning construction. I clearly remember standing on the old dirt road above the present site of Coulee Dam, looking down into the huge valley with the very small Columbia River flowing through at the bottom of the canyon. I remember Dad telling us that this would be the site of the largest dam in the world. There was some work going on, with crews drilling, laying pipe, and doing some of the preparatory work before the construction of the dam. Those jobs were stimulating the economy in that area and Dad was there to capitalize on these opportunities.

In those days a sign painter also had to be a salesman. Dad would go into a tavern, order a glass of beer, and engage the owner in conversation, pointing out how much better his business would be if he had a sign on his window and/or beautiful picture over the bar or on some blank wall space. I am sure that the skills he had learned as a mercantile clerk stood him in good stead insofar as selling was concerned. Dad was an excellent sign and pictorial painter and one of his specialties was laying gold leaf on signs that he painted on windows. This was the ultimate for merchant's signs and Dad was an expert in this now nearly extinct art. He could also paint any kind of mural the owner requested. In a tavern this would often be a mountain scene of pine trees and perhaps a large-antlered buck in the foreground. Some of his paintings were much more elaborate. I know of at least one of these minor works of art that still exists. It is on the wall of the Checkerboard Tavern on East Sprague Avenue, in Spokane.

My oldest brother, Bill, was the man of the house when Dad was out of town. He occasionally was pretty rough on Chuck and me, although I have no doubt that we needed a considerable amount of discipline.

On the other hand there is a sort of built-in discipline in a family that lives under those conditions. I think my children and grandchildren would have a hard time understanding the circumstances under which we were living. One would have to start with the understanding that the whole family pitched in to make a living. Almost all transactions were based upon some bartering. Dad traded sign work for the two-by-fours and lumber that were used to frame the house. We had no electricity, no running water, and the sole sources of heat were a wood stove and a wood cooking range. We got our water from a well, dug by Bill, that was about 100 feet from the house. The outdoor toilet, or outhouse, was about 150 feet from the house. We used kerosene and gas lanterns.

The farm fields produced modest amounts of timothy hay, alfalfa, and wheat. We had an old binder that, when Dad could get it to work, would cut and bind the wheat into bundles. These would fall out behind the binder and had to be stood upright and leaned together into "shocks" so the wheat would dry and protect itself from rain. I can recall one time that Dad took Chuck and me into the field and let us help shock the wheat. I can still remember the great sense of pride and joy I had in helping my father with the farm work. It was much more manly and much more satisfying than weeding the garden, cleaning out the barn, and milking the cow. This was man's work.

For thrashing, separating the wheat from these shocks, we depended upon a roving crew that went from farm to farm at harvest season. The men on these crews would thrash the wheat, sack it, and sew the sacks. It was an exciting time on the farm because the thrashing machine was run by a big steam engine, which had to be fed wood to make the steam. The men worked terribly hard from sunup to late into the night. At mealtime the thrashing crew was always fed by the family for whom they were working. This was no small chore, but Mother took pride in filling them up with excellent meals.

We had about 40 acres of timber on the ranch. In order to provide wood for the winter, trees would be cut down with a crosscut saw, bucked up into about 16-foot lengths, and skidded down into an area near the yard. The sawing procedure was something like thrashing time. A man came with a great circular saw that was run by a drum that was attached to the flywheel of an old Chevrolet engine. Everyone would work to push the lots onto the carriage and the sawyer would push the carriage forward and into the sawteeth, which was exciting to watch. The wood would then be split, generally with an axe or wedge and sledge hammer. Chuck and I were always glad to see the saw crew because if they didn't show up we had to do the same job by hand with a crosscut saw.

We survived mostly on food we produced, except for staples such as flour and sugar. I clearly recall that my mother made a bet with my father that she could feed the whole family for a month for $5. At the end of the month, the total amount that she had spent was not five dollars, but it was only $7.50 — for a family of seven!

I might add that the family was well fed. We had a large garden, as I well remember, because Chuck and I had to weed it. We had fresh fruits and vegetables during the growing season and plenty to put up for winter. I recall Mother never canned less than 200 quarts of tomatoes. She also canned beans, apples, and other fruits. We had a root cellar under the house for the purpose of storing potatoes, squash, and other vegetables that we raised in the garden.

We had hogs that generally lived off the slop from the kitchen, mixed with some grain that was raised on the tillable land of the farm. We always had two or three cows and as many as five cows at one time. Chuck and I had the responsibility for cleaning the barns, milking the cows, and taking care of the horses, all of which was done before and after school, which made for a rather long day.

Dad and Bill did the hunting and we almost always had venison. We had chickens for the eggs, calves for veal, and mother won many prizes for her homemade bread. I believe that our existence on the farm in Cottonwood was best described by the humorist Sam Levinson, who said, "We weren't poor, we just didn't have any money."

The first day that we went to school, Chuck and I, along with our sister Jean, walked the mile and a half to the Cottonwood Grade School with our lunches in hand. Jean caught the bus there and went on to the Chewelah High School.

The Cottonwood Grade School was a one-room structure in which one teacher taught eight grades. Before our move, I had just started the third grade and Chuck had just started the fifth grade. But in the one-room schoolhouse, there happened to be no one among the twelve or so students in the third or fifth grades. So Dora Johnson decided that we should be promoted, myself to the fourth grade and Chuck to the sixth. Chuck and I received this very well, since it provided us with the illusion that we had gotten out of a year of school.

Dora Johnson was about 23 years old and responsible for the whole school. There was no principal and no maintenance person. Not being a superwoman, Dora had more than her share of problems. She did her best, giving out different levels of assignments. But there was always an element of all the classes

Bob, me, Chuck, and Jean.

overlapping in an ambiguous way. It was difficult to figure out just how well one was doing.

Miss Johnson announced the opening of school, lunch, and recess with a hand-held bell. Lunch and recess were my favorites. The school was situated on about two acres of land. It had two outdoor toilets, one for the boys and one for girls, both equipped with Sears and Roebuck's catalogs. The playground had a teeter-totter, swings, and a few other bits of play equipment. Cottonwood Creek ran nearby and this provided a bountiful crop of native brook trout to anyone who thought to bring a pole and bait to school. I remember how amazed I was to see Paul Tate and a few others catch fish with their bare hands. They would feel under the banks with their hands until they located a fish and then whisk it out of the water. The fish were laid aside to take home after school for dinner. I enjoyed the Cottonwood School. Walking to and from school was an adventure. Learning from Miss Johnson was an adventure. Playing in the school yard was an adventure.

When Chuck and I got home, we did our chores of cleaning the barn and then were on our own. Chuck and I shared the ownership and stewardship of an old buckskin horse named Buck. Buck really was a workhorse, but we could ride him at our leisure and this brought both of us great joy plus a few lumps and bruises. One time I was riding Buck when he stepped on a rotten stump and broke open a large nest of yellow jackets. I was engulfed in bees and by the time I got home a half-mile away both my eyes were swollen shut. I'm sure this was the reason I became allergic to bee stings for the rest of my life.

Our other horse, Nellie, belonged to Bill, and Chuck and I were forbidden to ride her. Bill thought that Nellie used to be a racehorse and that she had foundered and had to retire. She was a beautiful yellow horse, weighing about 1,000 pounds, and she could run like the wind. Many times, in Bill's absence, Chuck and I took great joy in sneaking Nellie out of the barn or catching her in the field and taking her to the lower forty and running her as if we were racing. On more than one occasion brother Bill caught us riding Nellie, and then there really was the devil to pay.

The family always had dogs. One time when Chuck and I were coming home from school during a very cold spell of about 32 below zero, we stopped in at the Hayford barn to get warm. Ed Net, a hired man at the Hayford farm, asked us if we would like to have a puppy. We said that we certainly would and he reached into the litter of pups, picked one up, shoved the pup's butt up against the workbench, took a knife, and cut the tail off quite a bit too short. Ed handed us the puppy, which I put inside my coat, and we headed for home.

This was the first puppy that we could call our own. We immediately named him Sandy and he brought great joy to us for many years. Sandy was the offspring of a bulldog and an Australian shepherd. He had beautiful features, just about half-and-half, with a blunt nose and a square chest with a white diamond in the center. He was brown and tan in color and stood about sixteen inches high. As could be expected, Sandy became an inseparable playmate and companion to us. One time he evidently had some type of fit and was running wild, frothing at the mouth, and glassy-eyed. The fit soon went away but it happened a number of times. I learned later that it was probably due to worms, but there were few veterinarians back then. The family also had two great Airedales called Mutt and Jeff. Jeff was killed by a cougar when we were visiting Gommie's place at Cataldo. A rattlesnake evidently bit Mutt on the ranch. He crawled under the house and died.

Outside activities in Cottonwood were very limited. We lived six miles from the nearest real town, Chewelah, and almost never went there. We were three miles from the crossroads town of Valley and the closest store, a general store run by the Kulzer family.

We did have a battery-run radio and consequently could listen to "Little Orphan Annie," "Jack Armstrong: All American Boy," "Amos and Andy," "Walter Winchell," and so on. I was an avid reader during this time and I can remember many days and hours when I would read, upstairs lying on my bed, stories of Tom Swift, Huck Finn, cowboys and Indians, and faraway places. Chuck and I built a fort out in the woods and our imaginations ran wild defending it against imaginary Indians. Occasionally when we felt unappreciated for some reason we would announce to Mother that we were leaving home and sleep out in the fort.

The biggest social activity in Cottonwood was a dance held at the Grange almost every Saturday night. Helen and Jean were courting age and the two Ludeman brothers, Fred and Rich, would take them to the dance. This courtship had to surmount a number of problems because the Ludemans lived about a mile on the other side of the dancehall. The Ludeman brothers would walk to our home, walk the girls back to the dance at Cottonwood, walk them home afterwards, then walk back to their ranch, a total of eight miles, not including the dancing. Young love knows no bounds. The Ludeman brothers were very handsome boys. Rich and Jean seemed to get along especially well. The courtship ended pretty much when we left the ranch at Cottonwood. Neither of the Ludeman brothers ever married. One still lived on the same farm when I stopped by a half century later, in 1985.

Neighbor Alvie Sears was one of Chuck's and my favorite people. We always enjoyed the opportunity of running into Alvie because he would pull out a can of Velvet, some white paper, and let us roll a smoke. After the smoke he would give us a little bit of Spark Plug chewing tobacco, and while we didn't do it regularly, my recollection is that we rather enjoyed both smoking and chewing at our early age. Sometimes we didn't have to go more than a mile to "run into" Alvie.

Being a bachelor and a little mischievous, Alvie was more like a pal than an adult. A building on the Sears property had burned to the ground and it occurred to Alvie that the charred pile might have some things worth salvaging. He hired Chuck and me to go through the pile of charred wood and ash to pick up all the nails and bolts we could find. The agreement we made with Alvie was that we would fill a big brass kettle, probably about three gallons, for which he would pay us 25 cents. We went to work bright and early and worked diligently all day. But the nails and other metal were hard to get to. Toward the end of the day we realized we were not going to get the kettle full. I doubt if Alvie Sears ever expected us to. So we filled the bottom two-thirds of the kettle with rocks and brick and filled the top with nails. When Alvie came that night, we showed him the kettle. He was delighted. He gave us the quarter and we left for home. Chuck and I both knew what we had done wasn't right, but we felt what Alvie was trying to do wasn't right either. Consequently, we weren't too grieved from a conscience standpoint. Alvie was madder than hell when he found out what actually had happened. Then he thought about the circumstances and calmed down to a simple rage.

Tony Stroyan was a neighbor to the southeast and one of the most prosperous farmers in Cottonwood. He had cattle, a very good hay crop, and a prized bull. More than once Chuck and I were walking up the road to the Stroyan House when we spotted the bull pawing the ground, preparing to take after us. We would hightail it to the fence and leap over it just ahead of the bull. We were both really fearful of that bull, for good reason. Tony also had two of the most beautiful blue roan horses that one could imagine. They weighed about 1,200 pounds and they were a driving team. In the wintertime, when walking was difficult, Tony would frequently stop by the house and offer to take Jean, Helen, or Mother to town so they could shop. What a beautiful sight that team of horses was pulling a sleigh through the winter snow! Chuck and I visited Tony in Chewelah about 1976. He died about two years later. He was a truly great person.

The only time I can remember Chuck and I going all the way to the town of Chewelah on our own was when Alvie Sears asked us to go there to get him some smoking and chewing tobacco. It was about a twelve-mile round trip. He didn't offer to pay us anything for running this errand, but I imagine we assumed he would give us something, although I'm not sure Alvie figured that he would ever have to pay us for anything after the "kettle of nails" con. We walked to Chewelah, got the tobacco, and started back along the highway. While we were walking, we decided that the least Alvie would do for us was to let us have a little bit of the Spark Plug chewing tobacco we had fetched for him. We opened the bag and each took a big chew. Almost immediately a car stopped and the woman driver asked if we wanted a ride. Riding was better than walking, so we jumped in.

Unfortunately, we had not thought to spit before we got in the car. One would have to have the experience of chewing fresh Spark Plug chewing tobacco to understand why this was such a mistake. It expands the saliva and juice in your mouth faster than yeast. Of course, the lady that was giving us a ride wanted to make conversation with these two little barefoot waifs she had picked up. I couldn't say a word, because if I had, I would have spit tobacco juice all over the car. Chuck, being on the outside, was able to roll the window down and spit without the lady seeing. I remember how the woman tried to get me to talk to her for those next four dreadful miles, and how I would only shake my head yes or no, my cheeks bulging ever bigger with tobacco juice. Finally she asked me where I wanted to be let off and warned that if I didn't tell her she might just have to drive me all the way to Spokane. I still don't know whether she had figured out my problem. She knew the minute Chuck told her where to let us out, because the instant I got out I spurted out great gobs of juice and tobacco, then turned around and thanked her. Ironically, a couple of years later, when we moved back to the Spokane Valley, that same woman turned out to be my eighth grade teacher.

One particular experience with forbidden habits left an impression that lasted the rest of my life. The fence along our road produced an abundance of chokecherries. One of the few uses for chokecherries was the production of a rather sour wine. This was the era of Prohibition and my father liked to have a glass of wine, so he kept jugs of fermenting chokecherry wine on a special shelf in the kitchen.

One day Mother, Helen, and Jean had to go to Valley to get some staples, leaving us alone in the house. We decided to take the opportunity to sample Dad's wine. We took out a gallon jug and sampled it. Bob, now being about four years old, was old enough to know what was going on, so to keep him from telling we gave him some, too. We noticed our sampling had left the contents of one jug clearly lower than the others. We decided to drink down all the jugs evenly so as not to leave any clue any was gone. In the process we all got very drunk. I clearly recall doing some wild and crazy things that day. One of our exercises while under the influence was to take the wagon up to the top of the hill and come roaring down to the road. I made this wild trip several times and enjoyed it thoroughly.

The next thing I remember I was lying in the road with my two brothers in about an inch of our combined vomit. Mother, Helen, and Jean had returned and found us passed out cold. Believe me, there was hell to pay. Drinking chokecherry wine turned out to be a very serious offense in the mind of my mother and we were punished. We were probably punished physically, though Mom never did that much. I recall her sitting on the edge of my bed rubbing the head of one sick little boy. She put up a stern front but I sensed she was very happy that we were going to live. I was not entirely sure I would live for some time. I don't know that I have ever been so sick in my life. Chuck and Bob had the same experience.

In the fall of 1932, Chuck and I were busy building a goat cart. Somewhere along the line we had gotten the impression that someone was going to give us a billy goat, and consequently we wanted to be ready for that occasion. The farm was spawning ground for used parts and we were able to find two wheels and an axle. We worked on this cart ceaselessly until it was completed and it really was a beautiful goat cart. We even found some paint to glob on the boards. We would talk endlessly about how wonderful it was going to be when we got the billy goat to pull us around in the cart. The cart had 18-inch steel wheels and neat little shafts just right for a billy goat.

Unfortunately, the person that was going to provide the billy goat never got it and we were in the position of having built the cart before the goat, so to speak. About four miles north of our ranch, on the east side of Chewelah Valley, there is a mountain cliff about 1,200 feet high. It was common knowledge that there were a lot of wild goats on that cliff. Not having received the promised goat, Chuck and I determined that we were going to have to go to the cliff and catch one of the wild goats. We hitched up old Buck to the wagon and Mother fixed us a lunch. We took along ropes and were absolutely optimistic about catching a wild billy goat. We stopped and left Buck and the wagon at a farmhouse at the base of the cliff, then Chuck and I hiked up to the top. Just as we expected, finding the wild goats was not any problem, but getting within a quarter mile of them turned out to be an insurmountable problem. After a long, hard day of trying to lasso a billy goat, two very tired and disillusioned boys went back to the ranch, got the wagon, and drove back home.

Being optimists, we soon came up with a whole new plan to get a goat for that beautiful cart we had built. We decided we would cut wood and sell it to buy a goat. We figured we needed about $20 to buy the quality of goat we wanted. I believe kitchen wood was selling for about $1.75 a cord at the time. A cord of wood is a stack four feet high by four feet wide and eight feet long, so we would need roughly ten such piles. Every morning we went to the stand of woods at one corner of our ranch, used a crosscut saw to fell a tree around 20 inches in diameter, and then cut it into 16-inch sections. Then we split the wood with a sledgehammer and wedge into pieces ready for delivery for use in kitchen stoves. We worked tirelessly and joyfully for the dream of a billy goat pulling our cart.

We had sawed, chopped, and stacked an enormous pile, perhaps half the amount we would need for the goat, when my parents announced we were moving back to the Spokane Valley. When we left the farm I can still recall looking wistfully at those piles of wood and how they would have translated into a goat for the beautiful cart. We left the cart on the farm.

The time that I spent on the ranch seems like a time in my life that was capsulated and set aside. We arrived there shortly after I turned eight years old and left when I was about ten and a half. It was a time when I had absolutely no worries in the world. How could you beat it, being eight years old, going barefoot all summer, never concerned about clothes, and learning to be useful by performing all sorts of manly chores.

4

Schooling

D ad had traded equity on the ranch for a house on ten acres of land located at the east end of Spokane Valley in Veradale, Washington. The house, at Sixteenth and Sullivan, wasn't much. It was about 20 feet wide and about 30 feet long with a small shed in back. It did have running water, a shower, and a bathroom, and these were luxuries very much enjoyed by everyone, especially the girls. There wasn't enough room for the whole family to live in the house at the time, but Dad promptly set out to build an addition to provide bedrooms.

Sixteenth and Sullivan, in Veradale, was very rural at the time. We were a mile from the main road, known as Appleway (now East Sprague). The nearest store was at the intersection of Appleway and Sullivan, and kitty-corner from it was Hubbell's Service Station, which was owned by Dad's second cousin from Virginia. Our school, Veradale Grade School, was located at the intersection of Appleway and Progress. After school we often went to a little store across the street from the school run by Mr. and Mrs. Hultman, wonderful, generous Dutch people.

Helen still worked at the Crescent department store in Spokane. Bill had quit school during his first year at West Valley High and was working as a mechanic at a nearby airfield called Felts Field. He was crazy about aviation and overhauled airplane engines. Jean continued high school at Central Valley, graduating in 1935 to go on to Cheney Normal College (now Eastern Washington University) and getting her teaching certificate. Chuck had been promoted two whole grades in the Cottonwood school, not because of his academic prowess, but simply because of the school's limitations. Thus he entered Central Valley High even though he was two to three years younger than his contemporaries.

When I showed up for school at Veradale Grade School, I could not believe how large it was. I could not believe there was only one grade in each room and each had an individual teacher. There were around 120 students in the school. To me, this seemed like an enormous horde after the dozen or so in Cottonwood.

Like Chuck, I was given a convenience promotion in Cottonwood, so I dutifully reported to the principal of Veradale Grade School that I was in the sixth grade. The sixth grade class was deep into fractions. I had never heard of fractions. They were also doing long division and I had never heard of long division. I was so far behind the class that I was somewhat awed. I was concerned about not looking dumb and probably did a considerable amount of bluffing and/or winging it. I never would catch up with my peers.

I paid attention to girls but I had not reached puberty and consequently my love was more like worship than romance. I had a big crush on Betty Nichols and while walking her home one day I actually put my arm around her. I was probably shaking all the way home.

This was in 1933, during the height of the Depression, and in many ways our lives didn't change much in Veradale from that in Cottonwood. We still depended upon Mother's garden for much of our food, and Mom was quick to get a cow and put it in the small barn behind the house so we had milk. Dad opened a sign shop on West Second Avenue in Spokane. Consequently he was again gone for long hours, working diligently to try to keep the family fed and clothed.

All of us younger kids earned money by picking berries, beans, tomatoes, and cantaloupes, each in their season. I remember we got 25 cents a crate for picking strawberries. That was 24 boxes. For raspberries, we got 35 cents, but raspberries were much more difficult to pick. In the summer we would work from about 5 a.m. to noon or 1 p.m. This work gave us our first opportunity to earn money. We would then generally walk a little more than two miles (to a spot near the present freeway and Sullivan) to the irrigation ditch that ran through the area for a swim. Other times we went to the Spokane River, where there was a sandy beach on the south side of the river. We usually began a swim in the racing river water with a dunk in the "bathtub," a rock that had hollowed out and held some water. Then we would dive down to the bottom of the river, get behind the rocks so as to be out of the current, then pull ourselves from rock to rock until we had crossed the river. It was great fun and when we were through we walked the two-and-a-half miles home to dinner.

Transportation was a high priority in Chuck's and my life. We used to visit the Veradale junkyard regularly looking for bicycle parts. It wasn't long until we each had a bicycle and not one single part of those bicycles was purchased.

Veradale Grade School had a Scout troop. The scoutmaster was Duke Davis, a large-boned, angular sixth-grade teacher. He had just enough of a temper that everyone knew he was boss.

When he said "jump," our only question was, "How high?" Chuck and I enlisted and for the first time I discovered I could do quite well in organized activities. It was something where I started out even with other boys and being able to keep up gave me confidence. I completed Tenderfoot, Second Class, and received my First Class Scouting badge. I also earned merit badges for my Star rank. But for some reason the scouting program was stopped and I never did receive my Star rank. I had become really good at tying knots and ten years later in Navy boot camp I won the seamanship contest.

Scouting meetings were held at night. After the meetings, especially when the moon was full, we looked for mischief, like stealing watermelons or cantaloupes. This certainly didn't go along with the Scout Oath or Scout Law. We did it for the lark and for the watermelons. We never vandalized or destroyed anything important.

On Halloween we were more ambitious. The major accomplishment on that night was to tip over an outhouse. We would prowl the region looking for likely targets. Since owners of the outhouses knew this game, they generally kept a good eye on their outhouses. Consequently, it was an exhilarating challenge of stealth and diversion. Some of us would be appointed to create a diversion. If it worked and drew the owner's attention, the rest of the group would run to the outhouse and, with a great heave and a ho, tip the outhouse over.

Mrs. Cheney, the principal of Veradale Grade School, had her hands full controlling such children every school day. She was up to it, though, being about six feet tall and at least 180 pounds. She could just about tear your head off with her voice and a jerk of your arm. One day in the eighth grade, I threw a wad of paper at some kid up in the front of the class, and just as I let go Mrs. Cheney walked in the door and it hit her on the head. She immediately took me into her office and administered her rubber hose. She had me by one arm and was swinging at me with the hose and I was running around yelling as loud as I could. Despite my protest, I distinctly remember having rather mixed emotions about the punishment. I knew I had done wrong and should be punished. I also thought that there was something a little bit macho about getting punished by the principal herself. My mother didn't think it was so funny. I had black and blue marks all over my back from the shoulders to the middle of my knees. She called up Mrs. Cheney and told her off. I gathered Mrs. Cheney wasn't too impressed. I had the feeling she had written me off as a lost cause. I did graduate but I suspect it was partly just to get me out of her school. In any event I was happy to get out and looked forward to entering high school.

Nearly all the years I was in grade school, my oldest sister, Helen, had been working at the Crescent department store and saving her money. In the summer after my graduation from grade school, Helen drew out her savings and made the down payment on a new house for our family. The house had belonged to a prominent businessman, W.O. Douglas, and was a beautiful house by any standard. It had a large kitchen for Grace Williams, a lovely formal dining room, a sun porch, two bathrooms, and four large bedrooms. It had a large double garage in the back. Shortly after we moved in, Dad erected a small barn in the back of the garage so Gracie, as he called my mother, could keep her great love, a Jersey cow.

Moving into this house was a real step up for the Williams family. Compared to the Veradale house, this was a mansion. It was great for Helen and Jean because it was a suitably fine residence for two beautiful and eligible young girls to welcome suitors. Best of all to me was that it was just up the street from Central Valley High School, about a 500-foot walk to school rather than a couple of miles bike ride I was used to. It was like dying and going to heaven.

This was the summer of 1936, and the Depression was far from over. Nevertheless, Dad's business was doing fairly well, but it kept him working practically all of the time. Chuck and I were extremely busy, since we had two paper routes — the *Spokesman-Review* at 4 a.m. and the *Spokane Daily Chronicle* in the afternoon. We bought most of our own clothes and even contributed to the family finances. Both parents never gave us spending money because they never had it themselves. To the best of my knowledge, the only discretionary money I ever received from my parents was when Mother gave me a dollar to spend at the Natatorium Amusement Park on the occasion of my eighth-grade graduation party.

That fall I entered Central Valley High School with three definite liabilities. At thirteen (in October of that year), I was still two years younger than my classmates. I was short even for that age, five-foot-six. And I was still lagging behind academically. In other words, I was short, young, and dumb. My paper route, which entailed not only deliveries, but also collecting from customers, took most of my spare time, so my social life was nil. I was also naturally shy and wasn't "in" with any group or clique.

Between my freshman and sophomore years an amazing thing happened. I grew about six inches, to about 6'1". In addition, I became a very handsome young man. My social life improved by the quantum. Girls who never knew I existed suddenly found me interesting. When I recall the many times I stopped, over the objections of a panting, squirming girlfriend, I realize just how puritanical my upbringing was.

This growth spurt left me with only two problems, those of being young and dumb. I had never learned how to study, and with the arrival of social acceptance that began to seem even less important. I think I had the ability, but not the discipline. Subjects that I happened to like I could do well in. As an example, I took an agriculture class and became intensely interested in judging potatoes. I won the Spokane County Potato Judging Contest. I really knew my potatoes. Yet at the end of the semester I received a D in agriculture. I confronted Mr. Kaiser, the teacher, and he informed me that I was smart about potatoes, but that was about all. I was furious. On top of everything else, Kaiser was also our tennis coach. It just happened that Betty Barzee and I had won second place in the mixed doubles tennis championship. I couldn't figure out how a guy who was so good at judging potatoes and tennis could get a D in agriculture, but that is what I got.

My aunt, Marybelle Schmidt, had a rooming house not far from our home. She contracted with Chuck and me to calcimine her five bedrooms. We accepted her offer of $1 per room, knowing that we could do the job in a couple of days and we would not only be rich, but also very liquid. While we were having lunch that Mother had fixed for us one day — Aunt Marybelle didn't believe in feeding hired help — we noticed an old touring car out back in the garage. It was a 1919 Davis that had belonged to her husband, B.E. Schmidt, who had gone blind with cataracts ten years earlier. He had put the car up on blocks, where it had remained since 1926. Chuck instantly fell in love with the car and I had a premonition that I was not going to see my part of the $5 from Aunt Marybelle. Chuck asked Aunt Marybelle for the car instead of the $5 and she accepted with a huge smile, no doubt figuring she not only got the rooms painted but also a cleared-out garage. Being two-and-a-half years younger than Chuck, I had no say in the matter. Instead I owned half interest in a car that Chuck really thought of as his.

A 1919 Davis had no top, but that wasn't important to us. It did have a beautiful green finish, which was still in good shape. It had leather upholstery, four doors, and a continental engine. Soon after we finished our calcimine work, we returned to get our car. Chuck had me pump up the tires with a hand pump while Chuck put gas in the tank — the gas being borrowed from Dad's panel paint truck, almost surely without Dad's knowledge. Almost miraculously, the car started with the first or second crank. It immediately let us and the neighbors know that the Davis was without a muffler. As we drove away, Aunt Marybelle waved and smiled. She seemed very happy with the exchange.

During the ten or twelve years the car had been in storage, the rubber inner tubes had rotted to a state of considerable weakness. If the *Guinness Book of Records* had had a category for flat tires repaired on the road, the Davis would have won hands down. But it turned out, as Chuck had anticipated, to be a great way to meet girls, and also state patrol officers.

Joe Alley, my very good friend of seventy years.

I enjoyed my sophomore and junior years in high school. I did not turn out for eleven-man football because, though tall, I was still fifteen years old and weighed only 145 pounds. I played six-man intramural football and tennis, and boxed, none of them with great proficiency.

But I got along well with people. Though I entered my senior year at only 15 years old, with most of my classmates being 17 or 18, I was elected president of the senior class. It was a great boost to my self-esteem.

Then the roof fell in. It seems there was a section in the school constitution that precluded a person from holding class office unless he or she had a C-average. Sig Hansen, the principal, did his best to break this to me gently and put it in perspective. But it was just too much. It meant that not only would I not receive an honor duly voted me by my contemporaries, but that everyone would know it was specifically because I was stupid. When I first learned that I couldn't serve, I went out to the parking lot and sat in my friend Joe Alley's car and cried like a distraught mother. Principal Hansen came out and talked to me again. It isn't easy to be kicked out of the presidency of the senior class because of not having a C-average and go back to school, but I did.

The next day Joe Alley, my best friend since the sixth grade (and still one of my best friends as I write this), said he wanted to be my lawyer. He wanted to get the school constitution changed to allow me to serve as the class president. Joe happened to be one of the smartest kids in Central Valley High School. I figured it was a long shot, but I agreed. I still don't know how he did it, but the student body changed the constitution to allow a dumb person to hold class office, and I was reinstated as president of the senior class. It was a very happy occasion for Luke Williams.

The winter of 1936 was one of the worst in history. Snow, wind, drifts, and temperatures of 30 to 40 degrees below zero made walking our routes miserable and very nearly impossible. But we managed it. Our boss at the *Spokesman-Review* thought the paper should be like the mail and go through regardless of the weather.

In the spring I turned out for the senior play and was given the lead, opposite Marie Sandow, a beautiful red-haired young woman. I had to kiss Marie in the play and it was great fun. I recall that I kissed her several times after the play, and that was even more fun.

In May of 1940, a nice young lady who worked in the school superintendent's office informed me that I was not going to be able to graduate because I did not have any — none — science credits. After a long discussion, she agreed to check the records again, and, lo and behold, she found she had been mistaken; it appeared I did have the required number of science credits! I

When I was elected Central Valley student body president.

have always felt a debt of gratitude to this wonderful person, but I have not been able to acknowledge her help, and still will leave her unnamed. But Edith Wilson Haugen knows who the person is.

In June of 1940, Patty Persons, the class valedictorian, and I led 64 seniors down the aisle. Academically, Patty was first in our class. I was sixty-third. I had tried to date Patty on several occasions in our senior year, but she would never go out with me. I always wondered why. Just a few years ago, her brother, Dr. J.T. Persons, told me that their mother would never let Patty go out with me because she was sure that I would never amount to anything. Given the evidence at the time, I can't blame her.

We seated ourselves in front of the stage in the gymnasium. Patty made her speech and I made my speech. Everyone received their diplomas and my schooling was over.

5

The Navy

After I graduated from Central Valley High School in 1940, I really did not have any plans. I was 16 and probably quite immature. My mother, God bless her, who has always had a great influence on my life, wanted me to go to college. She made all of the arrangements for me to register at Cheney Normal College (now Eastern Washington University), which was about twenty miles away from home. I will never forget that she went down to Montgomery Wards and bought me a beautiful full-length blue overcoat so I would be well-dressed in college. It was one of the nicest things I have ever owned.

I enthusiastically signed up for courses in zoology and the like and then neglected to do any studying. Somehow I had never gotten the hang of academic study. One of my professors told me frankly that not only was I not going to pass, but it might be a good idea for me to try something else for a couple of years while I matured.

I left college after two quarters and went to work for Dad until I heard about a government job involving spraying fruit trees. The pear psyllid bug was eating up all of our pear trees in the Spokane Valley and the Pear Psyllid Control Department was responsible for protecting them. I applied and got the job, which paid 50 cents an hour, very good money as far as I was concerned.

Soon after I went to work, I met a self-made entomologist by the name of Harry Gross. Harry would later go on to start a very successful business in Spokane called the Northwest Seed and Insecticide. Harry and I got along just great. He soon took me out of spraying and made me his assistant in scouting fields for the pear psyllid bug. Harry gave me responsibilities and taught me how to find the bug. I have always felt that he had a great deal to do with my maturing.

As soon as I had gotten a little experience, Harry sent me to Wenatchee, an important fruit region in the center of Washington State. I was going completely on my own, at age 18, to conduct the United States government's pear psyllid program.

One problem was that I had exactly 35 cents in my pocket. I hitchhiked and ate only what 35 cents would buy for three days. In Wenatchee I had no money and no place to stay. I finally just went to a boarding house and explained to the landlady that I worked for the government and could pay her soon if she would put me up. The wonderful landlady said of course. It was like finding another home. I never will forget what it was like to eat my first meal in three days. Even though I had grown up in a poor family during the Depression, this was my first experience with hunger.

On Saturday night, Dec. 6, 1941, I went to a dance at Newman Lake with Chuck, Joe Alley, Fred Palmroy, and George Kallas. On the way home about 5 a.m. we heard the announcement on the car radio that the Japanese had attacked

*In search
of the pear
psyllid
bug.*

Pearl Harbor. We all naturally decided we were going to join the service as a group. But then my mother talked to me. She said that she knew that Chuck and I would probably have to go, but she would really appreciate it if I would stay and help the family as long as I could.

I stayed with the pear psyllid program. Harry sent me and a college graduate by the name of Joe Guy to Penticton, British Columbia to see if the bug had spread to Canada. I discovered the bug and soon the U.S. government dispatched a team of about 15 people to begin mapping its spread. Because I had discovered it, I was put in charge of these men. Some of them were graduate entomologists and therefore did not think a lot of this 18-year-old's authority. Nevertheless, I supervised them, and it was a great learning experience for me.

Meanwhile, I got word that brother Chuck joined the Air Force in August of 1942. With word that Chuck had joined I felt it was time for me to enlist. I already knew what I wanted to do in the service. My neighbor Jackie Berg was in the submarine service. When he came home with the Twin Dolphin symbol of submariners on his sleeve, I was stricken with hero worship.

I enlisted on my 19th birthday, Oct. 4, 1942, and got orders to report to Farragut Naval training station in northern Idaho. The morning I was supposed to catch the bus in Spokane to begin training I woke up a little late and was in a panic. Dad told me to take the car and leave it parked in Spokane and he would pick it up later. Speeding toward Spokane, I was stopped by a state patrolman, who said I must accompany him to Spokane to be issued a ticket. At the Spokane police department, an old police captain with a beautiful Irish brogue asked me routinely what my hurry was. When I told him that I had to catch a bus to take me into the Navy, his mouth dropped open. He turned to the state patrolman and said, "What kind of man are you,

With my dad as I headed back to Navy training in 1942.

that you would arrest a young man on the morning he is off to protect the country — *and the likes of you!*" Then he tore up the ticket and apologized on behalf of the state patrolman. It was a very satisfying send-off to my Navy service.

I did well in boot camp on everything except, predictably, the mathematics exam that was crucial to getting into any technical schools, such as submarine school. I scored 38 out of 100. But an instructor assured me all was not lost because raw aptitude would count, too. So I applied myself to every chore, and at the end of boot camp I succeeded in getting assigned to torpedo school in San Diego.

I really "turned to" in San Diego. The only thing I thought of was getting through torpedo school despite my self-knowledge of not being very successful in schools. I never went out the entire three months of the school. I stayed in the barracks and studied torpedoes. The day before the final examinations I came down with the mumps and was in great pain, but I did not go to sick bay for fear I would not get a second chance to take the test. During the test, one of the chiefs came back to my desk and looked all around. He was wondering if I was cheating because he had looked at the first part of my test and the answers were verbatim from the manual. I explained to him that I had memorized the manual.

I graduated second in the class. It was like potato judging all over again; I was the expert. What Harry Gross told me was true. You can do anything you really want to do. I felt good about myself.

The guy who graduated first, Gene Cerimelle, from San Francisco, and I were made torpedo instructors. This actually took me away from my whole purpose of being in torpedo school, which was to get on a submarine, but it was such an honor at the time that I did not think about that. As torpedo instructors, we got to go on shakedown cruises on submarines and destroyers. In the submarines, we experienced depth charges dropped by our own ships at various distances. The pounding knocked the cork off the walls. I loved it. Being on a destroyer when all batteries of five-inch guns are firing is another stunning experience.

On a shakedown cruise on the sub *Tullibee*, I met a third class torpedoman who wanted a shore assignment because his wife had come to San Diego. We applied to swap jobs. The submarine captain interviewed me and accepted me, but the torpedo school wouldn't take the swap because the other guy did not have an instructor certificate. It turned out a lucky thing for me. The *Tullibee* was sunk on her fifth war patrol and all hands were lost.

Tired of instructor school, I heard that the Navy was looking for torpedo specialists to form a battlezone service group. The Pacific Theater strategy called for Marines to take occupied islands and set up an airfield. The Fighters and Torpedo planes would then operate from it to take the next island. Since the airfield might be in operation while the island was still occupied by enemy forces, the special torpedo groups needed combat training. I applied and went through an intensive course that included small arms and commando training. About the time the training was done, the Pacific strategists discovered that the island-to-island strategy was not necessary. They could leap several islands at a time. That left my unit with no particular mission.

Finally in December of 1943 we shipped out from Portland, Oregon, headed for a forward base on Saipan. We were on a Liberty Ship. I took one look at my assigned bunk next to the ship's propeller and from then on slept every night on the deck. We went to Honolulu and the Marshall Islands. I will always remember the Marshall Islands because we had been at sea for a long time and when we anchored, they brought cases and cases of ice cold beer, which was greatly appreciated. We drank it on the deck and looked out at the islands, which were devastated by the recent battles.

I don't know how long the island of Saipan had been secured when we got there, but I was told there were only 17 Japanese prisoners out of the 30,000 that had recently occupied it. Japanese prisoners just did not surrender; these 17 were captured while unconscious, so I was told. I remember that when the Americans played baseball, these POW's sat at some distance sullenly watching the action. I happened to be nearby one day when a new Japanese prisoner was brought into the headquarters camp. The naval officer asked him why he hadn't surrendered earlier. He said he was afraid to because he thought he would be killed. He had planned to escape back to Japan. The officer asked him

Relaxing on Saipan.

how he planned to do that. The soldier said he intended to find a boat or raft and row back — about 1,200 miles!

Things were quiet on Saipan. Occasionally a Japanese airplane would fly over and drop a bomb, on the Emperor's birthday, or something. We had planes ready all the time and would get an intruder before he got very far offshore. Once I was at the torpedo station, near "Suicide Cliff" on the northern tip of the island, named because Japanese soldiers and civilians had jumped from it rather than surrender to Americans. Suddenly two Japanese fighter planes appeared on the horizon. They weren't 50 feet off the ground when they passed over me going toward the air base. If the Japanese pilots had known that where I was standing there were about fifteen warheads, each with six to nine hundred pounds of explosives, they might have bombed us and blown us and half the island away.

Except for such occasional incidents, life on Saipan was dull. There were poker games going on all the time because there was little else to do. On payday they would start out playing nickel-and-dime poker in the mess hall, and eventually the winners would end up in a no-limit game for all the money. I turned into a very good poker player. I was conservative. I wouldn't bluff. I remember one of the first big hands I ever won I had three fives, and that beat two pair for a pot of about $115. I couldn't believe there was that much money in the world. The big players tended to be the same people. Some people are just crazy gamblers and stayed in the pot too long. They liked to think they had more than they did. I noticed that some people bluffed when they shouldn't. I wasn't flamboyant and I didn't bluff. I bet a hand for what it was and if the cards weren't there I folded. I wasn't betting on luck. I was betting on facts. I sent my winnings to the bank at home.

I was still pursuing my dream of getting on a sub, but now I was aware that I had developed a new obstacle. My eyes were getting bad. Through one of my friends in the sick bay, I obtained the standard military eye chart and memorized the whole thing. When I took my physical I "read" every line of the chart the doctor pointed to. Finally on August 1, 1945, I got orders to report to the Naval Submarine School in New London, Connecticut. I was ecstatic. Not only was I going to get out of Saipan, but I would finally get to go into the service I had had in mind since I joined the Navy.

On my way to the disembarkment station, I had the jeep driver stop by the torpedo shack so I could say a few parting words to my commanding officer, including my guess of his heritage. This officer was hated by every enlisted man that had anything to do with him. One man set a booby-trap for the

On Oahu, shortly before discharge from the Navy, 1945.

officer that nearly killed him. We heard that the lieutenant's problem was that while he was away on Navy duty his wife divorced him and married an enlisted man.

I was at the Saipan disembarkment station on August 6th when we heard that the first atom bomb had dropped on Japan. The consensus was that this would end the war. The next day I got on board the *S. S. Robertson*, a destroyer. While we were en route to Honolulu, the news was broadcast over the ship's intercom that the second bomb had been dropped on Nagasaki. How quickly the whole war picture changed. It looked like the war would actually be over soon.

In Honolulu I reported for another physical before going to New London. The doctor asked me if I planned to stay in the Navy if the war ended. I knew this had some bearing on his recommendation, so I said of course I would stay in the Navy. He said to come back and see him in the morning for his final report. When I did so, he had re-enlistment papers waiting for me to sign. He told me, very sensibly, that it did not make sense for the Navy to send me to New London for training if I did not plan to stay in. I thanked him and admitted I was not ready to make that kind of commitment. In the last days of the war my dream of going to Submarine School had ended.

One problem that left me with was that my orders said if I did not go to New London I was to be sent back to Saipan, where I had just cussed out one of meanest officers in the Navy. As I was thinking about this, the barracks public address system announced they were looking for enlisted men to manage barracks for returning service men. Volunteers had to have a "right arm rate," that is, have the specialized training of a boatswain mate, gunner, or torpedo man. My commando training qualified me and after a ten-minute interview I was assigned as

Master of Arms in charge of Barrack 135 at the Aieha Separation
Center.

The only problem with this assignment was that the
Separation Center was 10 miles from Honolulu. So to avoid
being cut off from a larger social life, I decided I needed a car. A
guy on the submarine base named Don Thompson was anxious
to sell his car, but he told me he had one problem. He had a
Japanese girlfriend he would still like to take out in the car
regularly. If I could loan him back the car when I wasn't using it,
he would make it worth my while. For example, he said, did I
need eggs? His job was to take unused supplies off submarines
when they came back into port, and he had dozens and dozens
of eggs he could give away. I immediately surmised that if I
could buy bread and secure a hotplate or two, I could sell
unlimited numbers of egg sandwiches to the hungry Navy men
coming from remote stations all over the Pacific through my
barracks. Louie Sassano, my assistant Master of Arms, and I
went into the egg sandwich business and they sold like you
wouldn't believe. The Chief Master of Arms told me if I didn't
quit selling the sandwiches he would put me on report. I told
him I would quit selling egg sandwiches when he quit selling
ham sandwiches. I also told him that I thought we both would
be better off if he left me alone and I would leave him alone.
The deal was made and that solved the problem.

With business purring along, I turned many of the details
over to Louie Sassano and decided to restart my college career.
I found that I had developed a craving for higher education and
attended classes at the University of Hawaii two or three nights
a week. I can't recall what I studied, but I think it was journalism.

Life was good in those last few months of 1945. I was almost
disappointed to get my separation papers in January of 1946. I
came home on the *Lurelene* and took the train from San Francisco

to Seattle. I was efficiently discharged at the Bremerton Naval station on February 11, 1946.

For some reason, when I went into the Navy I never expected to survive the war. So many things about the war and my service were unknown that it always seemed to me the odds were that something would happen to me. Even when we crossed the old high bridge at the outskirts of Spokane, I felt that something was likely to happen, like the bridge collapsing, just to keep me from getting home.

But it didn't happen, and when the train rolled into the station, there were my father, my mother, brother Chuck, and little brother Bob. It was a homecoming and a very, very happy occasion.

Things picked up about where they had left off three and a half years earlier. Chuck had an idea for us. He had started a neon sign business and he wanted me to be his partner. He said everyone needed signs now that the war was over. He said we could make an unheard of sum of money painting, repainting, and selling signs. Chuck's company also just happened to need $600 to pay some bills, which I happened to have.

I put Chuck off to catch my breath. A day after getting home I put on my uniform and took the bus to Spokane just to have a look around. I will always remember that while it was homecoming to me, the people who had lived there were not the least bit interested in me or anyone else that was coming home. The war was over. People were getting on with their lives. I went back home and told Chuck I would go into business with him. We shook hands on my father's gravel driveway and the Williams Brothers Sign Company began.

6

Williams Brothers Neon Company

I did not plan to follow my father into the sign business. After leaving the Navy I was intent on going to college and becoming an entomologist and working with the United States Department of Agriculture. My other dream was to own a Chevrolet convertible that I had fallen in love with.

When I arrived home Chuck was already involved with the sign business. He had sold a neon sign to a local restaurant and he didn't have the $600 for the materials he needed to build it. Therefore, Chuck soon began trying to convince me to join him in business. He said Dad had been in the sign and pictorial business since 1907 and everyone knew of Luke Williams' signs. Chuck said Dad would be the perfect salesman and we would make a fortune. Chuck was very persuasive and it wasn't long until I became a willing participant. The closer it got, the less attractive four hard years in college seemed compared with the prospect of making money selling the signs businesses had been unable to obtain during the war.

A partnership is like a marriage without the benefit of sex. I believe it is no accident that so many very successful partnerships have been between brothers — the Wright brothers, the Dodge brothers, the Hills brothers, and so on. Family ties can help keep the relationship together. Chuck and I had been partners our entire lives and were destined to be partners the rest of our lives. But that is not to say Chuck and I always agreed. In fact, we had fistfights over our differences. I remember once we hadn't been in business together for six weeks and we got into a hell of a fistfight in front of my mother. The problem then and in virtually every other instance was money. I didn't think Chuck had any sense of fiscal responsibility.

In retrospect I can see one of the strengths of the Williams Brothers partnership was that we were so different. Chuck had inherited all of the genes that had made my dad risk everything in his search for the mother lode in mining. Chuck was a risktaker, naturally adventurous and imaginative. He was the type of person who invented the world — unfortunately, not always on the first try. He got us into more desperate spots than I can count. My job was figure how to get out of them again. I used to say that Chuck laid the eggs and I had the job of hatching them. I owe a lot of my successes to Chuck's initiative. I am absolutely positive that if he had not put me into many a difficult situation, I would not have risen to the occasion. I also know that if I had not risen to the occasion we would have been bankrupt more than once.

We were a perfect team in the sign business. Chuck was an exceptional pattern man and sign painter. He could make patterns and sketches that were just great. I brought the know-how of sign hanging and the grunt work to the partnership. Chuck would make the sketch and sell the signs, and I would oversee building, wiring, and hanging them. We both contributed greatly to the partnership. One thing we had in common was that we were both tireless workers. I'm sure we both got that from Dad.

It turned out Chuck had been right about prospects in the sign business. In those years following the war we could call on practically any business and find people who needed new or repainted neon signs. We used Dad's garage as our shop and his truck and ladders to install the signs. Our very first sign was for the Greenacres Cafe, located in the Spokane Valley not far from our home. Chuck designed it and we subcontracted construction of the sign cabinet to the Jensen Byrd Company of Spokane. That company's sheet metal department was run by a tobacco-chewing sheetmetal genius by the name of Shorty Lenz. We got the glass for our signs from Sid and Carl Carlson. Chuck made the patterns and I supervised our crew in painting them, putting in transformers, and installing the glass. One afternoon in the spring of 1946, we connected the wires of the Greenacres sign and, *Viola!* the Williams Brothers' first neon sign lit up. We were ecstatic.

Our natural market was Spokane, right at our doorstep, and the largest city in the region. When Dad sold a sign in Spokane, we found a business license was required. You had to have a $1,000 bond to get a business license, and we did not have the money. So we actually built our business in the many smaller towns scattered over the Inland Northwest. I sold several signs in Wallace, Idaho, the famous mining town that was also famous for its houses of ill repute. I remember once a very nice-looking lady came into our shop and said she wanted to buy a sign. Since we had already done a good deal of business in Wallace, I recognized her as a prominent madam by the name of Delores. She reached in her purse and pulled out cash, perhaps $300 or $400. I told her she only had to put down a deposit and could pay the rest on delivery. She said, "I pay for things just like I collect for them, in advance." Actually, Delores was a wonderful citizen of the city of Wallace. The Kiwanis Club named her citizen of the year because she provided uniforms for the high school band.

Me and Al Smith in front of the first Williams Brothers headquarters about 1947.

In the summer of 1946 we moved out of Dad's garage and rented a real shop at 808 North Lincoln in Spokane. The rent was $85 a month, a lot of money to us. About that time the Jensen Byrd Company had decided to quit their sheet metal business, so their two crack employees, Shorty Lenz and Dick Caufield, set up business with us in the new building and became our in-house cabinet makers. My brother Bill had been running a glass business in Boise, Idaho, but wanted to come back to Spokane. So we moved his operation into our shop. Suddenly we were a self-sufficient sign-making company. We were competing head-to-head with Electrical Products Consolidated, a very large and successful public company headquartered in Seattle, and we were eating their lunch.

That didn't mean we didn't have problems. In fact, the more success we had, the more problems we had, because every sign we sold had to be built with our own money. Electrical Products leased its signs to customers, so to compete we had to do the same. In the long run the fact that we leased signs rather than sold them outright would be a huge moneymaker. In the short run it meant we had to finance our customers' signs. Eventually the money would come to us, but in the short run we were always strapped for working capital and always a little late on our payments. I recall one day driving all the way to Orofino, Idaho, about 150 miles from Spokane, hoping to sell a sign to a tavern so we could collect the down payment and get it in the bank. I sold the sign and rushed back to the bank and made the deposit just in time. We always met our obligations, but spent a lot of time persuading bankers to let us have just a few more days to do so. Mike Nelson, the manager of the Seattle-First National Bank, told me once he had never made so many trips to repossess the same truck.

Our sign-hanging truck was a converted Army half-ton truck sold to us through the federal Reconstruction Finance Corporation. We attached a crane to it ourselves and Chuck painted it and created a logo so that it looked just great.

It was while I was seeking the loan on the Army truck that I met a beautiful young assistant in the adjacent Social Security office by the name of Bueletta Nordby. She had chestnut brown hair and a big smile. She was a college graduate and obviously very intelligent. I asked her to go out. I had to take her out in the company's old International pickup, but she didn't seem to object. We went out to dinner, went horseback riding, drove down to visit her parents, Rudolf and Mildred Nordby, farmers in the tiny town of Genesee, Idaho. We had a wonderful time. We got married on October 19, 1947. I borrowed Joe Alley's 1942 Chevrolet to go to California on a honeymoon. I had $45 and Chuck's assurance that he would send money as soon as he could collect it. Fortunately, Bea's parents gave us $500 as a wedding gift. We spent $250 on our honeymoon and saved the other $250 for a sewing machine. When we got back, we lived in a $35-a-month apartment over a grocery store with about three million cockroaches. I was very lucky to find a girl like Beauletta Nordby. Many periods in our lives I was working twelve hours a day, seven days a week. Yet she stuck with me for forty-eight and a half years, until her death in March of 1996.

It was at our plant on North Lincoln in Spokane that I learned about the steel, electrical, painters', sheet metal, and glassblowers' unions. They were all hard to deal with. The electrical workers were represented by a man by the name of Paul Kruger, who seemed to me as antibusiness as anyone you could ever hope to meet. He did not like business or business people, period. I had to join the electrical workers' union in order to be able to hang signs. The night I joined the electrical union I was told by Paul

Kruger that I could not attend the rest of the meeting, or any other meeting, because I was an employer as well as a working electrician. There is no question I developed an antiunion prejudice at this time. We were trying to build a business and create employment, yet we were treated as if we were against workers. Our business depended upon our being efficient, yet the unions forced us to hire people that were not necessary. I remember more than once taking a person out in the back alley and settling our union differences just before we came to blows.

Yet we were blessed with wonderful employees. Soon after we started Williams Brothers, I traveled to Idaho to look up an old Navy buddy, Al Smith. He lived in a cabin with a dirt floor, which I had never seen before. His mother was a wonderful person, and the cabin was clean as anything. I got him to come to work for Williams Brothers, but he was never happy so far from the woods and driving a caterpillar and he soon left. (As I write this, I still keep in touch with Al. In his 80s, he still drives a caterpillar across his 40-acre farm.)

During the short time he was with us, Al brought a friend, Willis Mackay, into the business. Willis was about 5'5" tall and weighed about 130 pounds. He married a woman by the name of June who was at least six feet tall and outweighed Willis by 80 pounds. Willis was absolutely infatuated with June and they had a long and happy marriage. Though small in stature, around Williams Brothers Willis Mackay was a giant. He was one of those people who could figure out how to do anything. Willis made sign cabinets, hung signs, wired signs, and put transformers in the signs. To Willis I attribute much of the success of Williams Brothers Neon Company.

Eddie Moran was a foreman for a neon sign company in Chicago that did subcontract work for us. I hired him away soon after I worked with him the first time. He was the type of foreman that every businessman loved— decisive, tough, and competent. He had a temper and he could stand up to a man that was twice his size. He seemed to be able to do anything and he did it on time and he did it right. Eddie got things done.

It was about 1950 when a very nervous guy walked into the Williams Brothers Neon plant, and said he was looking for a job. His name was Bob Wintermute. We hired him as a serviceman to our signs and on his first day at work he did something like twelve or fifteen service calls. We were very impressed and would never cease being impressed. Bob would be with the company for the next 30 years, finishing out his career as Vice President of Manufacturing. I gradually learned the source of his nervousness. During the war he had been a boatswain's mate on a mine sweeper. In the furious Battle of the Coral Sea, he was sunk five times. His first ship was sunk, then the ship that picked him up was sunk, until he'd had to abandon five ships.

This small circle of hardworking employees brought Williams Brothers Neon through the difficult first years of establishing a new business. They were also the people behind American Sign & Indicator, the much larger and more technical company Chuck and I were about to launch.

7

American
Sign and
Indicator

I n 1950 the Seattle-First National Bank announced that it was going to enlarge its Spokane branch. The building at Sprague and Howard would be doubled so that it extended to the corner of Riverside and Howard. This would give the bank a very prominent position on Riverside Avenue, the main street in Spokane.

Chuck quickly saw this as a great opportunity and challenge for our business. He figured that if we could sell the sign that went up on the new building it would make Williams Brothers the most prominent sign company in the Inland Empire.

The bank's name, "Spokane and Eastern," is a long one for a sign. To complicate that, the sign had to display the circular symbol of the Seattle-First National Bank. That was already quite a bit to put on a legible sign, but Chuck also insisted that the display should provide both the time and the temperature as a fitting public service for the most prominent new building in Spokane's downtown for decades.

Chuck showed me the first proposal he planned to put before the bank. It showed a 90-foot-tall vertical section of a sign with the bank's name and an electrical thermometer on the outer edge. Underneath the vertical sign was a circular sign that said Seattle-First National Bank and under that was a lamp bank with a time sign on it. Being the sign hanger and service manager, I was not completely thrilled with Chuck's "thermometer." The problem was that there would have to be 150 separate units of neon with a transformer operating every section to get a thermometer to go from 40 degrees below zero to 110 degrees above zero. We decided that having individual units of neon for each degree of temperature was unnecessary. This made me very happy as the service and hanging manager. I was also thinking of our service people hanging from a bo's'n chair three times a week changing transformers and neon tubes.

Chuck came back with his next design, which was a vertical sign with the bank's name in large letters and the Seattle-First emblem at the bottom. Below the sign he had a standard lamp bank to display the time and a separate bank to display the temperature. This design would show both the time and temperature constantly. This plan added up to an enormous sign, more than Seattle-First was likely to approve. As our discussions progressed, we evolved the idea of a single panel of lights that would show the time for a few seconds and then the temperature for a few seconds. This had never been done before, but we couldn't see any reason it wouldn't work.

The problems with doing it soon became apparent. Since they were electric mechanisms, you had to keep the time running constantly, although it was only displayed half the time. You also had to register the temperature changing every second, though you were only showing it on the sign half the time. This meant a rather intricate system of switching on and off. The switchings had to be reliable second by second, twenty-four hours a day, to build confidence, which was very important to a bank.

But we were still very excited about the idea. We called Ed Schulenberg, president of the Time-O-Matic Company in Danville, Illinois, the main maker of electric time signs. Ed said that he was soon going to be in Seattle and Chuck and I arranged to meet with him there. Ed studied our idea carefully, then finally pronounced his opinion that he could build the mechanism. But he didn't know why we wanted to, because if a person looked up and wanted to see the time, he might instead be shown the temperature, and this would be irritating. Ed was quite dogmatic. I imagined it would bother Ed to wait two or three seconds for the time, but I doubted it would bother most people.

We shook hands on the deal. Ed would make the mechanism for $835. Probably it was his doubts about the convenience of the clock that led him to readily agree to Chuck's requirement that we get the product exclusively. Time-O-Matic would make the mechanism only for Williams Brothers Neon. Chuck later had the good sense to go to Greek Wells, a Spokane patent attorney, and file a preliminary patent on the concept. I remember that because Chuck gave Mr. Wells $100 of our money, which was $100 I knew we could have used in a thousand other places. Chuck had the vision to understand that the simple solution to the bank's sign problem had great potential.

Chuck showed the design to the bank officers in Spokane and they got as excited about the idea as we were. In that era, bank signs were customarily limited to brass plates on the building wall displaying the bank's name and the date it was established. The officers of the Spokane and Eastern saw that providing the public service of constant time-and-temperature announcements would justify a 90-foot-high sign on their expanded building. We confidently promised them we would have this magnificent sign up and running by Christmas, though it wasn't built yet and in fact nothing like it had ever been built before.

While we were busy fashioning the new sign, the plant in Danville delayed delivering the mechanism. When they finally put it on an airplane to Spokane a week or so before Christmas, the airport in Spokane was fogged in and the airplane passed right over and landed in Seattle, 250 miles away. Chuck and I got in our Army surplus truck, drove to Seattle, claimed the crate from Danville, and drove back to Spokane. We opened the crate in our Lincoln Street shop and confronted the first time-and-temperature sign, an incredibly complicated mechanism. It was a 5-by-12-foot steel box filled with wires and relays that had to switch on and off by the second, interrupted by more wires and switches hooked up to a thermometer. This mechanism would be attached to the bank of lights we had built four feet high and twelve feet long. I took one look at it and thanked the Good Lord that we had a person by the name of Willis Mackey to make it work. We all worked around the clock for days. About 4 p.m. Christmas Eve, 1951, I was dangling above Spokane's Riverside Avenue, connecting the 90-foot-tall sign to the bank. We switched it on that night and it worked perfectly. That is, it worked perfectly for a little while, until one of its many mechanisms broke, and I went up the ladder again. Years later, when the time-and-temperature sign began to catch on, our competitors would tell potential customers not to buy it "unless you want a ladder up in front of your building 24 hours a day." There was some truth in that in the early years.

But the sign was an instant hit. Everyone in town could see it looming over the street. Everyone glanced at it to find out if they were late or just how cold it was. It has been determined that at least 80% of the people in the area will read the time and temperature sign. This readership is eight to ten times more

Our company built this seven-story high sign in 1951. It is remarkable for being the first alternating time-and-temperature sign in the world. It was installed on the Spokane and Eastern building at Howard and Riverside in downtown Spokane. (From the Ray Fisher Collection)

than that of a plain plastic sign, and it builds top-of-the-mind awareness—the ultimate goal of all advertising.

The Spokane and Eastern sign itself was beautiful. The faces were maroon porcelain with cream lettering. It became a landmark in Spokane until the bank was torn down 25 years later. Other banks in Spokane were envious and eventually could find no other response than to order similar signs for their own buildings. The president of Spokane and Eastern's major rival, the Old National Bank, told an amusing story about the sign while introducing me at a Kiwanis meeting. He said he was meeting with a client and remarked the weather was coolish. "Yes," the man said, "I noticed it was 37 degrees down at the bank," — by *the bank* referring to Old National's main rival, the Spokane and Eastern.

The sign was such a success we immediately organized the American Sign and Indicator Corporation in 1952 and became specialists in the "double-T," as we referred to the time-and-temperature mechanism. From the reaction to the Spokane and Eastern sign, we never doubted we had a saleable product. We kind of thought it would sell itself. It didn't work out that way. We found bankers are naturally conservative and needed some convincing to spend so much money. This was especially true of banks that were managed from a far-off headquarters where the street appearance of local branches was of little concern. The benefits of the sign were much easier to sell to local owners who walked past the bank every day, as customers did. This was true in Montana's decentralized banking system, and it was in Montana, going from small bank to small bank, that I learned how to sell time-and-temperature signs.

One problem in convincing bankers to buy the sign was that we were a brand-new company selling a very complicated technology. Now our custom of leasing rather than selling signs became a major selling point. The bank wouldn't have to risk the full price of $12,000 to try the sign, but just $364, the cost of a month's lease. To reassure them that the technology worked, we put in a "performance clause" that said if the sign was ever out of operation for more than 36 hours the rent stopped until it was fixed again. I remember when Chuck and I told one of our bankers, Frank Guse, about the performance clause. Mr. Guse was flabbergasted that we would ask him to finance a contract that became worthless if we couldn't fix a mechanical problem in less than two days. Finally he said reluctantly, "Well, boys, I know you did this in the best of faith, and the buyer is a good customer of ours, so I am going to finance this contract." But what, he asked, would we do if the next customer demanded such a guarantee in their contract? Chuck said without hesitation, "Why, we are going to bring it right to you, Mr. Guse." The old man almost burst. He said if we ever brought another performance contract to him to finance he would have us thrown out of the bank. Luckily, Mr. Guse didn't run the entire bank. He had a loan officer by the name of Dick Stejer who was friendly to us and became a big help.

The performance clause was a tough business condition. But ultimately it made American Sign and Indicator the place to go for anyone who wanted a time-and-temperature sign. A time-and-temperature sign has got to work all the time or it is an embarrassment. We quickly gained a reputation for standing behind our work — because we had to. Our guarantee that the sign would work never changed. If our mechanics couldn't get a sign working, I put on coveralls and went there personally. Years later I remember getting a call from a sports arena in Houston saying they were having a lot of problems with their sign. I called our vice president in charge of maintenance. He said, "Luke, we've tried, and we just can't seem to fix that sign." I said, "Bill

(Justice), if you can't fix that sign you can't fix the other 1,000 of them." He fixed it. I don't know how. He might have given them a new sign or he might have spent a ton of money. But he fixed it.

The guaranteed performance policy was expensive and risky. Problems with signs were not always our fault. But I am convinced this policy saved the company. About 1955, when American Sign became a big money-maker, Ed Schulenberg, who built the mechanism for us, successfully challenged our patent. (Years later an attorney told me we had lost the case through a small error. Our attorney did not establish that the money we had paid to Schulenberg had paid for engineering as well as manufacturing). The invalidation of the patent meant that any sign company in the world could compete with American Sign & Indicator Corporation in building and selling time-and-temperature signs. But by then we had established an unchallengeable reputation in the business. Schulenberg never did reap the rewards that he thought he was going to get by invalidating our patent. Even the mighty IBM tried the business and gave up because they could not compete with us. Because of our reputation for service, people who wanted time-and-temperature signs wanted to deal with AS&I.

In the early years, American Sign and Indicator had the same problem that had plagued Williams Brothers Neon. Selling leases required us to put up the capital to build the signs, and we didn't have the capital. The more successfully we sold, the more broke we were.

Someone suggested we try to get financing through the federal Reconstruction Finance Corporation, a federal agency that helped small businesses that could not secure regular financing. A kind, fatherly gentleman by the name of Arthur Chase listened to our story and authorized a loan of $100,000.

We were so naive that we thought it was the solution to all of our problems. We soon discovered $100,000 wasn't nearly enough to nourish a rapidly-growing business. We went back to RFC, but the head of the agency, another sympathetic man by the name of Mr. Greene, said the agency had loaned all they were authorized to. (Much later Mr. Greene told me that Charlie Parks, manager of the Spokane and Eastern Bank, had told him that we were bankrupt but we didn't know it). Mr. Greene said, though, that he knew of a man in Walla Walla, a small town in the southern part of the state, who was looking for high-risk investments. Mr. Greene offered to introduce me to the man and I said please do.

As Mr. Greene and I drove to Walla Walla, Mr. Greene told me that the investor, Mr. Sherwood, would want a third of the company as a bonus for financing the company. I stopped the car and said that would be impossible. After thinking about the alternative, which was bankruptcy, though, the impossible became more palatable to me and we continued our journey.

I met Don Sherwood and his brother, Cameron, and liked both of them from the start. Don Sherwood agreed to a $150,000 capital loan and to finance our ongoing contracts, which the RFC could not; this was worth the same as $10 million, in our desperate condition. Don drew up the deal and I initialed it. That was the beginning of a great association between the Williams brothers and the Sherwood brothers. They gave us the chance we needed to show what a profitable business American Sign could be. Not long afterward, the Spokane and Eastern bank reconsidered and decided it did want to finance us. It offered a much lower rate than the high-risk money of Don Sherwood, and so of course we had to take it. Chuck and I went to Walla Walla to tell Don. He was not happy about it, but he was always a gentleman, and soon he had us over to his house for an amiable dinner. Don Sherwood's timely loan of $150,000 returned him a profit of $8 million when the company was sold twenty years later. I learned a lot from Don Sherwood. I had a lot of respect for him because he was an honest and honorable man.

From the time we took on the Sherwoods as our new partners, we did not have serious financial problems again. It was wonderful. We could concentrate all of our efforts on manufacturing and selling the Double-T.

8

Developing a Sales Format for AS&I

From the time that first sign went up on the Spokane and Eastern Bank it was the talk of the town. We knew we had a wonderful product. We had dreams of this changing the look of every bank in the country and we immediately set out to exploit the opportunity. We went to Art Madsen Advertising, a prominent firm in Spokane, and they made a beautiful brochure that showed the sign in its entire splendor on the front page. Inside it gave a description of the Double-T. The brochure explained the benefits a bank could gain by sponsoring this public service.

We sent these out to selected states and got a good response from certain states, usually those with bank systems which encouraged local ownership. The best response was from Montana and I was assigned to go sell them. When I started meeting with bank presidents, I found more reluctance than I had expected. Buying a time-and-temperature sign was a very big decision for a bank. The time-and-temperature sign cost $12,000 minimum besides the rest of the display and leased for $364 per month. While the idea intrigued them, they hung back and thought about whether it was the right thing to do. We discovered we had a whole new challenge in front of us and that was to learn how to sell this new product.

The first thing we did was to redefine the Double-T display from a sign into an advertising medium. Not many bankers ever thought of paying $300 or $400 a month for a sign. On the other hand, that wasn't much to pay for advertising. Everyone within sight of the sign looked at it, and when they looked at the time or temperature, they also looked at the bank name on the same sign.

To speed up the decision-making in banks, I developed and announced the policy that we would sell only one sign in a small community. We signed a "temporary franchise" with a bank that would seriously consider buying a sign. This really helped because the person who signed the temporary franchise knew he had time to consider the product, but if he did not buy the product the bank's competitor probably would. It confronted the manager of a small bank in Montana with the opportunity of a lifetime.

Still there always seemed to be some reason why a bank couldn't buy right now. Our first sale, after the initial sign in Spokane, was to the Metals Bank and Trust in Butte, Montana. The bank president, Mr. Frizzel, wanted the sign but had the problem that one of his biggest customers was in the sign business himself, and he would resent the bank working with someone else. I told the bank president that we could solve the problem by making the local sign man, Fred Ackerman, a partner and have him assemble and hang the sign. Frizzel doubted this would work, but he told me if I could get Ackerman to go along the bank would buy the sign. I went to see Mr. Ackerman. He actually laughed at me when I asked if he would work with us. He let me know I was nothing but an out-of-town soap salesman in Butte. He assured

Demonstrating the earliest computerized mechanism to control an electronic sign (about 1960).

me the Metals Bank would never have anything to do with me. I told him I kind of thought otherwise. If I were right, would Ackerman be willing to make the sign? I made it a dare. He scoffed and repeated I wouldn't get anywhere with Metals Bank. But if I did, I asked, would he help build our sign? Sure! he said sarcastically. Why not! It wasn't going to happen anyway.

I thanked him politely and went back and told the banker that Mr. Ackerman said he would build the sign only if the bank bought it. I got a signed agreement and headed back to Spokane. The next day Mr. Frizzel called me and asked if I "heard Ackerman." He said when Mr. Ackerman heard about the deal on the sign he shouted loud enough that it should have been audible in Spokane. I laughed. I knew that Ackerman would cooperate anyway, specifically because he was so proud. He had given his word and he stood by it. He built the sign.

An old established company called the Electrical Products Consolidated, based in Seattle, had begun selling its own version of the Double-T. We had the technology and the record, but Electrical Products Consolidated, EPCON, had the prestige of a well-known name. I ran into the manager of EPCON in Great Falls, and he wanted to talk to me. He talked and talked. I told him a couple of times I was due in Havre, at the far eastern edge of Montana, to sell a sign. When I finally got free and drove to Havre, I discovered that the EPCON's sales manager had been there the whole time, talking to the bank president I was scheduled to meet with. While I was being detained in Great Falls, EPCON sold the Havre bank a sign! I was so mad that I sent the bank president a wire pointing out that we had a patent on the technology and would use all legal means to stop EPCON from exploiting it. If his bank wanted our technology, I said in the wire, it should buy it from us. The bank president called me in Spokane, more because he was mad about the wire than anything else. But we had a good visit. I told the man he could save himself a lot of potential problems by buying from us. He finally agreed and signed a contract with AS&I. We eventually sold him several signs for banks he owned.

In the early days, Chuck and I would go out on the road for as long as six weeks at a time calling on banks and learning how to sell time-and-temperature signs. In between we would talk endlessly about what sold signs. When Chuck returned to mind the shop, I continued traveling through Montana and other Western states (often with Bea and baby Brenda in her crib). It was a good education for me. I kept careful track of what worked and what didn't. Every time I walked out of a meeting with an unsuccessful conclusion, I would stop and ask myself what I had done wrong. What could I have done to have gotten the bank to understand the great benefits it would achieve by sponsoring or buying a Double-T from us?

It was in Montana that I began to develop what I called my "Ten Step Advertising Sales Call." The lessons weren't so cut-and-dried as that name suggests. There weren't exactly ten of them, for one thing. They were general lessons we learned about selling our product and they became standard within the company.

Our first rule became: Never give a sales presentation unless you are talking to the decision maker. After talking with many vice presidents and advertising managers, only to discover they had not in turn managed to persuade the higher-ups, I determined never to give presentations unless I was satisfied I was talking to the person or group that could actually make the decision to buy. Otherwise, I was leaving the sale of my sign in the hands of an advertising manager who might or might not do a good job of selling it and who in any case was working for someone else. If you weren't talking to the decision maker you might just as well be talking to the moon.

Getting to the decision-making group was often difficult. I don't know how many banks I walked into, talked to a receptionist or secretary, who then made a call and informed me the president was unavailable. I concluded the only power a secretary has is to say no, and so it is better to get appointments through the mail with a brochure, through mutual friends, or through referrals from other customers.

The best referral was from a bank that already had one of the signs. We encouraged potential customers to call existing customers. This is where our expensive maintenance guarantee paid off. If you could get a president of a bank who was considering a sign to call the president of a bank that had one, you would have one of the best salespeople in the world working for you — for nothing.

I learned the value of persistence from a particularly frustrating experience in those early years. We had a lead from a savings and loan association in Sterling, Colorado. To make my presentation, I flew to Omaha, Nebraska, rented a car and drove almost all night to Sterling, getting stopped for speeding on the way. I arrived at 4 a.m., caught a couple hours' sleep, and called the chairman of the bank. He was obviously embarrassed to hear from me and told me that the bank's board had met the day before and decided against the time-and-temperature sign. Needless to say, I was disappointed. I argued that I should at least have a chance to make my case. Since it was a small town, I said, maybe the board could get together again — even if to turn the sign down a second time. The bank president was a genuinely decent person and he decided to try to help me make my presentation. He managed to get the board together for a second meeting. I had lunch with the board and then I gave one of the best presentations of my life, showing slides of the bank in Sterling as it was, and how other banks with the sign looked. After the presentation, the board voted again and reversed its decision. It would lease a sign.

After that meeting, one of the board members stopped me and said, "Mr. Williams, I have never seen a better sales presentation in my life." He said he found it especially remarkable that whenever a board member asked a question, I responded to him by name. How could I do that, since I had just arrived in town? I explained that I had asked the bank president to identify each person during lunch. I could remember the names because I had taken a Dale Carnegie course that taught me to recall names by associating them with something visual. I have since lost most of that ability, but I know it was great fun to start a response to a stranger's question by saying, "Yes, Mr. Brackle, I agree. . ."— by imagining he ordered "brackle-li" for lunch or that he's sitting at the "brack" of the room.

I always went into a sales presentation armed with what I called my "photographic survey." This was a number of photographs I had taken of the outside of the bank. When I set these photos in front of executives, and then added a picture of a bank with our sign attached to it, I could almost hear them thinking how much more noticeable their bank could be with the sign — or, on the other hand, what would happen if their competitor got the sign and they did not.

I soon got a chance to test my Montana procedures in a much larger arena. All of our business had been in the West and we decided it was time to expand eastward. Bea, my wife, and daughter Brenda (who was about five years old) and I moved to Chicago to open a Midwest office. We rented an apartment at the Rogers Park Hotel and I opened an office in the Chicago Board of Trade Building. The office had a desk, a telephone, and cost $35 a month, including sharing a secretarial pool.

These proved to be the hardest six months of my professional life. It wasn't easy to convince anyone to buy a very expensive, very technical electric sign from an unknown company located in Spokane, Washington. In my mind all my frustrations are summed up in the experience with the Gary National Bank in Gary, Indiana. It was one of the first leads I had gotten after arriving in the Midwest and with great excitement I drove to Gary. I was working with a vice president by the name of Jackson and we got along fine, but Mr. Jackson apparently could not convince the owner of the bank, a Mr. Glasser, to buy the sign. I ended up going back to the bank at least 40 times. Finally I got an interview with Mr. Glasser himself, and the first thing he demanded to know was why he should buy my time-and-temperature sign for $14,500 when he could buy an IBM clock for $12,000. I laid out my literature and proceeded to answer his question by explaining the time-and-temperature advantages. While I was doing so, he turned his back on me and looked out the window. I had been frustrated when I came in and that finally broke my patience. I picked up all of my things, put them in my briefcase, walked over to his desk and said: "Mr. Glasser, you are not saving $2,500 by buying the IBM sign. You are wasting $12,000, and you do not strike me as a person who has ever wasted a nickel in his life." And I walked out of his office. To my surprise, he followed me out of the office, apologizing. "Now Mr. Williams, don't get in a hurry," he said. I just kept walking and he followed me clear out to the street. There he finally said if I would come back Monday, Mr. Jackson would be waiting for me with an order for the sign.

That was how I sold my first sign in three months of trying in the Chicago office. After that I quickly sold signs to the Ohio Citizens Trust Company, to the Mercantile Bank in West Chicago, the Twin Cities Savings and Loan Association, the Omaha National Bank, and the Security Bank in Kansas City, Kansas.

When I sold a sign to the Ohio Citizens Trust Company in Toledo, the response was so overwhelming that the bank became great boosters of the sign. Marvin Wilkenson, a vice president of the bank, and I became good friends. On his advice, I hired an agency in Toledo which, for just $500, polled people near the sign and found that more than 80% of them glanced at the time-and-temperature sign. That became a key fact in our sales presentation. One day while in Chicago, I received a phone call from Bill Scott, chairman of the Federal Sign & Signal Corporation, a New York Stock Exchange company. He said he would like to meet me. I made an appointment to go to his office. When I entered he asked, "Where are your feathers?" I asked what he meant. Bill said his sales people had told him an Indian from Spokane was in Chicago; his staff had assured him that the "Indian" would get no sales. "But I see that you, Mr. Williams, have sold six signs in the Chicago area and my staff has sold none." He wanted to know my secret of success, how I did it. I said, "It's very simple Mr. Scott. Your people say at the end of the lease your company will give them the sign. I say at the end of the lease, 'Why would you want to own it?' because all time and temperature signs require ongoing maintainence."

With such prestigious banks displaying our sign, we were finally established east of the Rockies and no longer an unknown company from Spokane, Washington. I hired a couple of salesmen to run the Chicago office and Bea, Brenda, and I packed up and left the Rogers Park Hotel and returned to Spokane. I was proud of my accomplishments while there, and had learned about selling signs in a whole new league.

It was Chuck who suggested we reduce the benefits of Double-T to a film. In 1957 we commissioned the short film that summed up the advantages of the Double-T sign in just six or eight minutes. After that our sales approach was complete. We trained sales personnel to begin by making the photo survey, to get an appointment with the decision-making group, to show the film, to answer questions, and to ask for the order before they left. On the basis of this formula, American Sign and Indicator Corporation grew to become one of the best sales organizations in the sign industry. We found we could get ten leads through advertising in periodicals, make seven sketches from those ten, and, with the right presentation, get four orders. It happened consistently. The Ten Step Advertising Call is one of the things I am most proud of in my life. It was the basis for selling $500 million of very expensive, very complicated time-

and-temperature displays to financial institutions all over the world. It was the formula of success for the American Sign & Indicator Corporation.

We never totally got rid of the problem of good, well-intentioned salesmen thinking they could take shortcuts in this presentation and still end up with an order. Salespeople tend to be very self-confident of their abilities to talk people into something. They think they can sell the product if they sell themselves. Usually they would come back empty-handed and puzzled about why no one wanted the product. They were needlessly repeating the learning curve I had gone through in Montana. Even the best salesperson in the world needs the experience of hundreds and hundreds of failed sales presentations to develop a method of presenting a particular product.

Aside from the formal presentation, every salesman has a sales approach. One of our best salesmen, Joe Siberz, was a schemer. He loved to drink Manhattans and plan ways of persuading people to purchase time-and-temperature signs. Yet he was also a genuinely likable guy and reliable friend. He used contacts better than any person I have ever known. He became friends with customers he was selling to, and stayed friends with them. They repaid him many times over by giving him good recommendations and leads for other potential customers.

On the other hand, some of the best sales people we ever hired came from the ranks of our field-service employees. George DeFrieze was a tobacco-chewing supervisor of one of our maintenance crews before I tried him out as a salesman. He learned to use the ten-step method and became a very successful salesman for us.

The lesson to be learned is that once you find how to sell something, you have to incorporate it into a format so you can teach ordinary people how to sell the product. People don't buy things because they like the salesman; they buy things because they believe that the product or service is going to help them in some way. All that is necessary is to effectively and efficiently show them how it will help them. The standard in the selling business is that people buy things they need from people they like. I always told our sales staff to learn how to tell the Double-T story in a professional manner, and be nice.

Most of the great product sales in America have been based on the solid footing of value and warranty. I know of no instance in the history of American business where people built a sales organization based upon mouth wrestling. It might be possible to trick or charm some people into buying something sometimes, but the approach is not consistent enough to sell the whole output of an entire company. To do that a sales force must have discipline.

I can think of no better example of what discipline can accomplish than the case of Jim Moran. Jim was a giant of a man. He was 6 feet 7 inches tall, weighed 270 pounds, and had a stomach as flat as an ironing board. He had been a football star at the University of Idaho and at the time we hired him was a lineman for the New York Giants. With his black Irish eyes and Fu Manchu mustache, he could look mean as hell. Jim would smile, but not often. A grin to meet people was a full-fledged smile to Jim. Sometimes, his eyes filled with crystals of blarney, and then he seemed like a lovable little boy.

We needed someone to help us get into the business of building scoreboards for major league football, baseball, and other sports stadiums. Our sales manager, Bob Weymouth, hired Jim to do that. Jim didn't take much interest in the job. He apparently thought AS&I was a nice place to get a salary, a car, and expenses while he entertained himself during the off-season. We received sizable bar tabs from him, but very few orders for stadium scoreboards. It was not long before Bob Weymouth figured out the whole sports scoreboard initiative was not working and he told Jim we were going to let him go.

I am sure Moran would have shrugged this off and found a more comfortable off-season job as a football celebrity if he had not injured a leg about that time. After surgery, one of Moran's legs ended up about an inch shorter than the other and his career as an NFL football player was over.

It was a big shock for him, but he faced it like the man he was. Jim called and said he wanted to come to Spokane to talk to me. When he came into my office it was like hearing a confession. Every bad thing I had thought of Jim he readily confessed. He had been taking advantage of AS&I, he said. But now that he was through with football, he had a wife and four kids to support. He wanted another chance.

Maybe he was conning me and it was okay if he was. At least he wasn't giving up. I told him if he wanted to work, we had work for him. But not as the head of the scoreboard division. He could work in our Los Angeles office, under the supervision of our very competent manager there, Joe Blumel, and prove himself by selling signs.

Then I began to explain to Jim all the things we had learned about selling AS&I signs. As I explained these lessons, I noticed

that his eyes were following my eyes every minute of our conversation. That was the first time I realized his great talent. Jim Moran was good at being coached. All of his life as a football player he had been knocked on his butt and then had to listen to someone tell him why it happened, and how to avoid it the next time. Those black eyes followed my every move and

Jim Moran

expression. I never saw a better pupil. Jim Moran was learning how not to get knocked on his butt again.

In Los Angeles Jim worked harder than anyone on some frustrating projects and he succeeded. After a few months in Los Angeles, he called me and asked if we could meet again. When I met him in Reno, Jim told me he had a plan for getting AS&I back into the competition to build sports scoreboards. For two days he laid out his strategy, and at the end of our sessions I rehired him as Sports System Manager. He had the same job as before, but he was an entirely different person.

Jim threw himself into the work and initiated the sports scoreboards division, which would become one of AS&I's biggest businesses. If AS&I is more famous for anything than the time-and-temperature sign, it is the big scoreboards thousands of excited fans watch second-by-second during football, baseball, and many other sports. We built some 250 college scoreboards for football and basketball. We built most of the Major Leagues' scoring systems from 1956 onwards. AS&I built the scoreboards for the 1984 Olympic Games in Los Angeles. Jim Moran played a big part in these accomplishments.

I will have to digress a little and tell how stadiums get multi-million dollar scoreboards. Sports people, especially stadium sports people, are a cult of their own, sort of like circus or carnival people. They like their own kind of people and don't like other kinds. Ex-football star Jim Moran was one of their kind. A college or professional team does not buy its own scoreboard. They depend upon sponsors to put up the money, and so potential sponsors are the people the salesman deals with. The team gives the salesman a letter authorizing him, for a period of about 90 days, to find sponsors willing to pay the cost of the sign. This is the salesman's hunting license to find sponsors.

Finding sponsors is no easy task because a scoreboard is not the best advertising buy in the world. It costs a lot of money to put that sign up in front of a relatively small audience a few times a year. Most advertisers would just as soon skip the honor of being a sponsor — except for one problem. If they say no and their competitor says yes, the president of the company or the chairman of the board might go to a game, and when he looks at the score, he finds himself looking at a competitor's logo. Avoiding that embarrassing moment was our best argument for a company's investing in an expensive scoreboard. We learned quickly there is little prospect of financing it without engaging the competitive spirit of advertisers.

Jim Moran became a great salesman because he understood competitiveness. Proof of that is a story I heard about him from a very trustworthy source. Jim was in a meeting with the advertising manager of Phillips Petroleum Company. He explained he was trying to sell sponsorship rights to the Oklahoma State University football stadium. Jim told the advertising manager he thought Phillips might be interested in providing the $250,000 cost, since he knew that the chairman of the board of Phillips was an Oklahoma State alum.

The advertising manager took down the information and told Jim he would get back to him. Jim said he had an appointment at Kerr-McGee Oil Company, a Phillips' competitor, at four that afternoon. Jim explained he couldn't delay it because a private airplane was waiting to take him to the Kerr-McGee headquarters.

The advertising manager got worried and called in a vice president, who listened and said it would take some time to get the executive board together. Jim said there wasn't much time because if he met with Kerr-McGee — at 4 p.m — he could not, as a gentleman, turn down any offer they might make. The vice president of Phillips called the president out of a meeting and introduced him to Jim. The president of Phillips Petroleum said he had a strong sense that they would like to sponsor the sign. But the expenditure of that much money was a matter for the board of directors. Jim said he needed a commitment.

The president was mad as hell about being put under that pressure, but he called the chairman of the board, the Oklahoma State alum. At 1:30 p.m. the chairman opened a meeting of the board. The chairman said, "Hell, we have a quorum of the executive committee, let's do it. We can't let Kerr-McGee sponsor the Oklahoma State scoreboard!" The committee voted and at 2 p.m. Jim shook hands with the chairman and thanked him. But Jim added that he needed to leave with a check for $250,000. The chairman exploded, saying there was no way anyone could get a check for a quarter of a million dollars on such short notice. Jim said he understood, but without a signed check he couldn't honestly tell the Kerr-McGee people — the people, he said again, that he had to meet at 4 p.m. — that the sign was truly sold.

The exasperated chairman called the corporation treasurer to prepare the check and rounded up a few more board members. They voted again and the president and chairman both signed the check and turned it over to Jim.

I know this story because, years later, when I was chairman of the National Association of Manufacturers, the chairman of Phillips Petroleum told it to me personally. He was still a little mad, but also impressed by Jim Moran's determination. There's room for Diamond Jim Bradys in business, and Jim Moran was of that type.

Jim became quite wealthy as a businessman. He supported his four children, one of whom, Rich, went on to play professional football for the Green Bay Packers. Sadly, Jim Moran died suddenly at the young age of 52.

9

Entry into Politics and the Goldwater Campaign

Through the 1950s business consumed nearly all of my time. What time I had left was taken up by a young family. My beautiful daughter Brenda was born in 1950 and my handsome son Mark was born in 1956.

Gradually, though, we brought the new business under control. By 1958 AS&I could afford to hire a sales manager to take over some of the work I had been doing. For the first time since I got out of the Navy, I had time to think about activities beyond business. I decided to volunteer in the campaign of Lloyd Andrews, a conservative Republican who was running against the liberal Democrat governor of Washington, Albert Rosellini.

My father was a Virginia Democrat, so I was probably a disillusioned Democrat. The first time I voted, in 1944 in Saipan, I voted for Franklin Roosevelt, whose leadership I saw as essential to winning World War II. But after ten years in business I had begun to see the connection between business and politics. Our company had five unions to deal with. The unions were very strong and very arbitrary in terms of what they would allow their members to do or not do. They could make the rules because they were very much politically involved in the Democratic Party. Since the Democratic Party controlled the state legislature, the State Labor Council had absolute control of business in Washington state. I had never met Lloyd Andrews when I volunteered to help him, but I hoped the election of a Republican would restore some balance to the rules businesses like ours had to follow.

Polls showed Andrews was winning two months before the 1960 election. At that point the AFL-CIO's national organization, Committee on Political Education, better known as C.O.P.E., became very active in the campaign. In September they started a massive advertising campaign against Andrews that was shocking, totally negative, and untrue. Their advertising in the newspapers and on radio cast Andrews as everything that was evil. They said he was against Social Security, unions, even education, though he was at the time superintendent of the state's public school system. The advertising was absolutely ruthless and mean-spirited. Because of the unlimited amounts of money C.O.P.E. spent, Andrews lost the election by 17,000 votes. There is no question in my mind that C.O.P.E. was responsible for defeating him. They did it entirely through a mud-slinging campaign, never letting the truth hurt a good story. This was my first experience with a major political campaign. I had never imagined politics was so negative and slanderous. While I had gotten involved in politics as a concerned businessman, the ruthlessness of the C.O.P.E campaign against Andrews shocked me into becoming a dedicated campaigner for conservative causes.

At that time, Barry Goldwater, the Republican U.S. Senator from Arizona, was a leader in the right-to-work movement in the country. I wrote to him and asked to meet with him about my experience in the Andrews campaign. He invited me to stop by his office the next time I was in Washington, D.C., and I did so. Barry Goldwater was handsome, suntanned, and lean. He did not have the "polish" I imagined in a national politician. He was a very blunt-spoken, rough-hewn, ordinary person, with lots of interests beyond politics. He was an experienced pilot and as soon as he discovered I flew a Navajo twin engine airplane, he wanted to talk about that. We hit it off immediately.

The Senator was not surprised about what I told him about C.O.P.E. and the Andrews campaign. He explained it to me this way. He said that 34% of the people in America go to the polls to vote a negative feeling. The strategy of the unions was to bring out all of the negative voters they could to vote against Republicans. He said that the negative vote against Republicans would give Democrats an edge of 2 to 5% of the vote in any election, and that edge had given Democrats control of Congress for the past 30 years. He said the Republicans and Democrats had an understanding that they would mutually avoid negative campaigning. The Democratic Party would generally adhere to its campaign pledge. But unions were not bound by the pledge and would spend millions of dollars demonizing and vilifying the Republican candidates. This would consistently bring out a negative vote that would be the margin of victory for Democrats.

I never heard a better explanation of American political dynamics. It was confirmed to me over and over during the next four decades, as I observed and took part in many campaigns. I saw that the Democratic campaign strategy exploits the divisions in America by preaching class against class. It is not usually the candidates who do it; it is the Democratic spokesmen such as James Carville, Lanny Davis, members of the Democratic National Committee, and others. But the Democratic candidates benefit from the demonizing of these unscrupulous people. The unfortunate thing is that it works and has worked for forty years. In the 1998 Congressional campaign, Democrats used people such as Carville to demonize all Republicans, saying they are against education, social security, welfare, and women's rights. They convince voters that Republicans are against all things that are good. Then when they take office, they reward all the groups that joined in this propaganda with tax dollars for their programs, with legislative favors, with personal promotions, and with social programs aimed at selected portions of the population. One good example of this is the donation of $2 million by trial lawyers to the campaign of President Bill Clinton. When Clinton was elected he stopped the tort reform proposed by Republicans. Stopping tort reform meant billions of dollars to trial lawyers.

The French writer Alexis de Tocqueville, who studied American-style democracy in 1831, predicted that democracy would work until the day that the American people realized they could vote themselves largess from the people's treasury. It seems to me that is exactly what has happened. The original Roosevelt Democratic coalition has expanded over the decades to include hundreds of political organizations such as the National Education Association (NEA), the trial lawyers' associations, minorities, women's rights organizations, and others that want to control Congress so it will vote largess from the public treasury to their causes.

The number one cause for liberals is welfare. As I write, the number of out-of-wedlock births is almost one out of four — 23% of all U.S. births. The actual number is about 600,000 per year. Liberals expect the taxpayers to pay for, in effect to adopt for life, these children. Aid to dependent children has become a cottage industry that has increased the cost of government unbelievably. Beyond the cost of supporting out-of-wedlock children, there is the heavy cost of law enforcement and incarceration that results when children are not taught self-discipline and responsibility within a family. Not only is each out-of-wedlock child doomed to a life without the normal emotional and economic support of a family, but it will cost the public billions of dollars to provide a poor substitute for these. The bill goes to hard-working, responsible people who would not think of asking their neighbors to support them. I remember in 1969 the total federal budget was $212 billion. As I write in 2001, it is over a trillion dollars. Liberals will fight any cut because expenditure on welfare benefits is their primary connection to their constituency.

I should explain my definition of a liberal and a conservative. In my opinion, liberals believe in government enterprise rather than private enterprise as an economic system. Government enterprise is just plain socialism like that in many countries in Europe. Liberal socialists are willing to give up many of their freedoms to receive political benefits from their elected representatives. Conservatives are people who believe in private enterprise and individual freedom. They believe individual freedom is the mainspring of all human progress. This is what our Founding Fathers believed. The fifty-seven people who signed the Declaration of Independence — many of whom lost their farms and their belongings in the Revolutionary War — were willing to sacrifice to attain the greatest economic system that the world has ever known. Liberals forget that the American economic system of free enterprise has produced more wealth than any other system known to man.

Soon after we lost the Lloyd Andrews campaign, I volunteered to be eastern Washington chairman for the Dick Christensen Campaign against Senator Warren G. Magnuson in 1962. Magnuson was, at the time, one of the most powerful political figures in the country and very popular in Washington state. On the other hand, Christensen was almost the perfect candidate to oppose Magnuson. He had the natural political touch of a Bill Clinton, but he was also a conservative Lutheran minister of perfect character and a great public speaker. Christensen lost the election by only 40,000 votes. On my side of the state, Christensen won the vote handily and carried 19 of 20 eastern Washington counties, which was a shock to the Magnuson forces.

The next year, 1963, I was at the annual state Republican convention and State Senator Sam Guess asked me if I would assume responsibility for the Draft Barry Goldwater Campaign in the state of Washington. After participating in two state campaigns in four years, I really thought that I had been spending too much time in politics and should get back to business. I told Sam that I would have to reluctantly decline.

When I went home I told Bea that I had been asked to run the Goldwater campaign but had declined. She was very disappointed. She said, "Here is a man who epitomizes everything that you believe in and I can't understand why you are not going to help him." I reflected on this and a few days later called Sam Guess and said that I would be honored to chair the Washington state campaign for Goldwater.

I flew to Chicago to meet with Senator Goldwater and other top supporters of his campaign. After the strategy sessions, Goldwater had a brief meeting alone with each of us. In my session with Goldwater, he told me that he had never wanted to be president and that he would probably lose the election. But he said he had promised so many people that he would head a genuinely conservative movement that he couldn't back out. "I've gotten in so damn deep," he told me, "that if I don't run it'll be the end of the conservative movement." He said he didn't expect a Republican could win that year because of the emotional aftermath of the assassination of President Kennedy. But at least

With Barry Goldwater, his wife and son. The occasion was the launching of Goldwater's campaign for president, which may account for Goldwater's grim look. He had confided to me that he didn't really want to be president.

if he made a good effort he would keep the conservative spark alive.

I knew that getting the Washington delegates for Goldwater would not be easy. Mort Frayn, chair of the Washington state Republican Party, and Janet Turtlelot, vice-chairman, were both from Seattle and Republicans more of the Rockefeller stripe. Mort had firm control of the state Republican apparatus and I doubted whether he would permit Washington to cast its votes for Goldwater.

When I began promoting the Goldwater candidacy among top state Republicans, many people assured me they would give Goldwater their support. But I was pretty certain that at the state convention I was due for a surprise. I decided I had better find out what the real situation was. I happened to own a small market research company called the National Research Agency, which was based in Chicago. I had this office send out a poll to all Washington state county Republican chairs asking them whether they supported Goldwater, Rockefeller, or Scranton for the nomination. Enclosed in the survey was a ballot and a stamped envelope for return. People didn't have to sign their name to the ballot, but the envelope was marked with a code so we could tell which county the ballot was from. The results were just as I suspected. Most people were for Scranton, including many who had privately told me they were leaning toward Goldwater. The chair of Spokane county, for example, always told me she was a strong supporter of Barry Goldwater, but when her ballot came back she declared for the Scranton forces.

There was no way Barry Goldwater was going to win the delegates of my state as things sat at that time. Mort Frayn declared for Nelson Rockefeller and he had firm control of a great majority of precincts in the state. I recognized it would be impossible to change the minds of most of the precinct people at that late date, but I had a strategy. Washington state had about 900 precincts, but only 516 of them actually had Republican precinct chairs. We would go out and find precincts that did not have chairs, find a Goldwater supporter in that precinct, and get the county chairman to name the person as precinct chairman. If we got enough Goldwater chairs at the precinct level, they could elect Goldwater people to the state convention, and the convention would in turn elect a Goldwater delegation to the national convention.

We were quiet about this at the precinct and county level, and by the time we got to the state level we had enough state delegates to allow us to elect all 23 Washington delegates to the national convention. This came as a total surprise to most of the party officials. When George Weyerhaeuser, a member of the famous timber family and a friend of mine, saw what was happening, he came to me on the floor of the convention and argued that the Scranton forces had to have at least some delegates in the interest of party unity. I made a deal with George that, on the promise that all would support the national candidate, whoever it was, we would agree to elect three delegates for Scranton. They were Mort Frayn, Janet Turtelot, and John Hauberg. They all went to San Francisco and worked hard to get the nomination for Scranton. But when they came home, rather than work for the nominee, Goldwater, they all resigned their posts.

The 1964 Republican Convention in San Francisco was historic. Until that time the liberal wing had controlled the Republican Party. Most people thought the battle was between the candidates of liberal Republicans, Nelson Rockefeller and William Scranton. But Republicans in other states had been active, as we had, and Goldwater was nominated despite the wishes of many of those who had been in charge of the party.

While I was on the convention floor, I had several calls in my hotel room from a Mr. Theodore White. I had never heard of Mr. White, but Bea had heard of him. She told me White was the author of *The Making of the President*, the book about the 1960 election. She insisted I call him back. White came to our hotel room equipped with a tape recorder and wanted to know in detail how we had managed to get the Washington state delegation for Goldwater. He was fascinated by our strategy of winning the Washington delegates by starting at the precinct level. In his best-selling book, *The Making of the President 1964*, White described our campaign in detail. White wrote: "The people whom Williams organized were people who felt, as he did, that the Republic was in danger — people willing to go up and down the street ringing doorbells to find their kin-in-spirit. . . . By June 11th to 13th, when the counties had sent their delegates to the state convention to choose 24 national delegates, the Goldwater people, under Luke Williams, controlled the state convention lock, stock, and barrel." White wrote that I had become the "dominant figure" in Washington's Republican Party, but: "It is impossible, on meeting Luke Williams, with his brown, thinning hair, his round face, his earnest eyes, his two-tone plastic eyeglasses, to think of him as a dominant figure." White thought I looked more like a high school principal than an important political figure. I have always taken that as a compliment. White described my politics like this: "Williams' philosophy is the philosophy of an honest man who has made it on his own, by wit, ingenuity and hard work; and the government that hampers him as his efforts flourish seems a hostile one. In Luke's philosophy, as he explained it to me, 'police protection, fire protection, and sanitation and education at the local level — these are the basic things government should do. But we've gone dangerously beyond these basic things, and the government needs pruning back — that's my concept.'" White was famously a Kennedy liberal, but I felt he did a fair and honest job of characterizing our campaign.

Many states had had conservative uprisings like ours and Barry Goldwater won the nomination easily. But most liberal Republicans refused to work in the election to get a conservative elected. In my state of Washington, the chairman and vice chairman of the state party resigned rather than work for Goldwater. The one national political figure I know of who worked loyally for Goldwater was Richard Nixon. I was with Nixon on a campaign swing through western Washington state, and at campaign stops before industrialists and unions alike Nixon argued energetically for election of a Republican. For all his faults that would be revealed later, I will always love Nixon for that.

The 1964 presidential race was the first time the Democratic National Committee had really resorted to unadulterated demagoguery in campaign advertising. The Democratic National Committee developed television ads that were despicable in their distortion of Senator Goldwater's views. One of the commercials against Goldwater hit so low that it is still shown in documentaries about politics to illustrate the beginning of the era of distortion politics. The commercial showed a little girl walking in a field of daisies picking flowers. The peaceful scene is suddenly replaced by a picture of a nuclear explosion, followed by a reminder to vote against Barry Goldwater.

Goldwater lost the election, but he achieved the minimum goal he had set for himself, which was to keep alive the spark of the conservative movement.

10

Politics and Business

Lyndon Baines Johnson was elected President in 1964. In his inaugural speech he announced the "Great Society" theme, which was an offer to let everyone benefit from other people's money or the public trough and really launched the first major effort at socializing America. It was absolutely opposite to everything I had worked for in supporting Barry Goldwater.

Almost everyone would be affected by the Great Society by the time it was all over, but one aspect affected me quite personally. Johnson's wife, Ladybird, wanted to do something "good" for America, since she was in the White House. Her dream emerged in the form of the Highway Beautification Bill, which was an effort to eliminate or minimize all outdoor advertising on major highways and freeways.

Of course, this was a big problem for the outdoor advertising industry. But Lyndon Johnson was a powerful person, and he was working with large Democratic majorities in both houses of Congress. The Outdoor Advertising Association of America, under the guidance of Phil Tocker, a very experienced politician, moved to minimize the effect of Ladybird's legislation.

One section of Ladybird's bill would have specifically prohibited electronic signs, including time-and-temperature signs, if they could be seen from a freeway or major highway. Since it was along such highways that major development was occurring, this could well have closed American Sign and Indicator Company and put its 900 employees out of work. The National Electric Sign Association asked me to carry its objections to Washington, D.C. I was happy to do so, since I had not only a philosophical objection to government regulation of business, but a very personal stake in the legislation.

The person in charge of the federal sign legislation was, of all people, Senator Warren Magnuson, the Democrat from my home state I had worked so hard to put out of office just two years earlier. I was pretty sure that Magnuson would remember me. A Spokane friend, Joe Drumheller, had told me that he was with Magnuson on that election night in 1962. Joe told me that when the Republican votes started pouring in from our side of the state, Senator Magnuson, who had been in the Senate since 1944, was extremely agitated. "We thought for awhile we were going to lose the Senator," Joe told me with a laugh.

Nevertheless the legislation as written would have been devastating to AS&I. I had no choice but to go back to Washington, D.C., hat in hand, and lobby the man I had almost unseated. I really was frightened as I headed for our appointment. I thought he might greet me by saying, "So you wanted someone else for your senator, huh?" Or I thought he might let me go to Washington and then at the last minute cancel the appointment.

Senator Magnuson greeted me at the door and I could not believe how cordial he was with me. He asked me questions about what was going on in Spokane. He wanted to hear all about my problem and assured me he would see to it. He was very proud of his influence in Congress. He had a copy of the federal budget on his desk and he tapped it and said, "Luke, they don't start any meetings without me." At one point his secretary came in and said, "Senator the people from Boeing are here," and Magnuson said, "Tell them to wait. I'll be a few minutes with Luke."

After the shock wore off, I realized I was witnessing why Senator Magnuson was such a successful politician. Whoever I had supported in past campaigns, he now saw me as a constituent, one of the major employers in the second largest city in his state. I'm also sure that he felt that if he did me a favor I would be less active in anti-Magnuson politics in the future — which I was.

After I explained the impact of the proposed sign legislation on the time-and-temperature business, Magnuson pushed a button to call in Fred Lorden, his chief of staff on the Commerce Committee. Magnuson said, "Fred, Luke has a problem. He has a good business in Spokane and we want to help him." I thanked Senator Magnuson as profusely as one could imagine and left with Lorden. Fred took me down to his office and asked me for more detail about the problem. I told him the Ladybird Johnson Highway Beautification Bill was likely to kill the time-and-temperature business. "What do you want us to do?" he asked. I replied that I would like public information signs, like time-and-temperature signs, exempted. Fred shoved a yellow writing pad toward me and asked me to write that down. When I gave it back to him he said, "That's fine," and told me he would take it right down to the room where the bill was being drafted and get the change made. When the sign legislation finally passed, sure enough, time-and-temperature signs and electronic public-information displays were exempted. Phil Tocker of the Outdoor Advertising Association could not believe what I had managed to do. The exemption saved the entire sign industry a lot of grief. It saved my company, American Sign & Indicator.

The same problem came up fifteen years later, in 1979, but it was more serious this time. The environmental movement had gotten a lot stronger, and it did not like signs or outdoor advertising. It especially did not like signs that burned electricity. Senator Stafford, chairman of a committee on environmental affairs, sponsored a bill to outlaw the signs near federal freeways and his committee had sent the bill to the floor of the Senate with a "do pass" recommendation, which almost always results in a bill's being passed.

I contacted the other Senator from Washington, Senator Henry Jackson. "Scoop" Jackson was one of the most powerful Democrats in that era. He had nearly won the presidential nomination in 1976. I went to Washington and once again explained to him that the passage of that legislation would very likely ruin one of Spokane's fastest-growing businesses. This time, I was not speaking to a stranger. Scoop Jackson and I were far apart in our ideas of government (less so on foreign policy, since he was very anti-Communist), but we were nevertheless good friends. When Bea and I made our first trip to Hawaii in 1957 we stayed at the Hawaii Village Hotel founded by Henry Kaiser. It happened that Jackson's suite was next to ours. We were with Jackson and his fiancee on several occasions, including a cruise on Mr. Kaiser's catamaran yacht. (Among the others on the cruise was the singer Andy Williams.) My wife, Bea, was a hundred percent Norwegian, as Henry Jackson was. This formed a mysterious bond between them and they became fast friends.

I have a feeling that what Jackson did to help me out twenty years later he did partially because of his fondness for Bea.

I contacted Denny Miller in Jackson's office and, as I had in Magnuson's office, explained that the bill as written could well cripple American Sign and Indicator, one of Spokane's biggest employers at that time. I asked again that the legislation exempt public service-type signs. Miller did a wonderful job of getting the Stafford Committee to entertain an amendment. Senator Stafford allowed the amendment strictly as a favor to Senator Jackson.

After the vote on the amendment, Jackson took Bea and me to lunch in the Senate Dining Room. He graciously waved off

With Bea and our old friend, Senator Henry Jackson of Washington state.

our profound thanks. But at the end of lunch he said, "Luke, I want one thing from you." "Anything, Senator," I said in my grateful mood. "Please get off Tom Foley's case." Young Congressman Tom Foley represented my district in Spokane. Before he went into politics himself, Foley had worked for Jackson and the senior senator was Foley's mentor in politics. Since Foley was a Democrat representing my rather conservative district, I had made a kind of hobby of trying to unseat him. But I had said "anything," and from that day forward I never contributed to another campaign against Tom Foley. I never explained why to those who asked for contributions and many fellow Republicans were puzzled. But I had promised. Foley, of course, became Speaker of the U.S. House of Representatives in 1989 and served until he was defeated in 1994. Whatever our political differences, the fact is Tom Foley was a wonderful man and a great American. After his defeat he was appointed Ambassador to Japan and served the United States very ably.

As a conservative Republican I have opposed many Democrats, but on a personal level I have worked with and liked many in the opposition. In fact, a Democrat helped me win the only political office I ever sought—a seat on the Spokane City Council. I only ran for this office because I was at the annual Blue Back Fish luncheon at the Spokane Club, and I happened to sit next to Neal Fosseen, who had recently been elected mayor of Spokane. At this luncheon I began explaining to Mayor Fosseen all the problems with the city. He said, "Well, Luke, if you don't like what is going on why don't you run for the city council and have a say in it?" Running for political office had never entered my mind, but I accepted the challenge and filed for the city council in 1962.

I was extremely busy with AS&I and did not have any time to conduct a political campaign. In my legislative fights against unions I had met a Democratic legislator from Seattle by the name of Bob Perry. He was an agent for the electrical workers in Seattle and a Democrat. It seemed to me his leanings were far left, if not socialist. Nevertheless, he and I got along just great. I admired his knowledge of politics. I think Bob Perry knew more about how to win an election than anyone I had ever met in my life. I told Bob that I was going to run for the city council and because business was so demanding I did not have much time to campaign. I think he was quite flattered that I asked for his advice. He told me the most important thing was to communicate my message to voters in a very personal way. He advised me to simply write a letter to all the people who had voted in the previous election and tell them why I was running. The letter simply would say, "Dear John or Jane Doe, my name is Luke Williams and I am running for the city council and I want you to know why I am running. I am very much in favor of limited government, lower taxes and I believe in economic development for jobs. If you agree, please vote for me." I wrote and sent the letter. Though I spent very little time campaigning, I won more votes than any other local candidate, including Del Jones and Don Bell, two very popular incumbents.

The business was going strong at the time and I really probably should not have run for the city council. I'm sure there must have been some motivation that intrigued me about politics. I don't think there's any doubt it was my experience with the Andrews-for-Governor Campaign and the Christensen senate campaign, in which I got the living hell beat out of me. To get so involved in politics you have to have a motivation, and I really believe that except for the experience of those two defeats I never would have gotten so involved in politics. Politics is a game where there is no second. You either win or you lose. If you win, you should win on the basis of what you believe in, and if you lose you should understand why you lost. I had lost two campaigns in quick succession and from that point on I was a very matured opponent.

In these years the Washington State Legislature was dominated by Democratic majorities that sometimes reached two-thirds. This allowed the most liberal wing of Democrats to control legislation without the help of conservative Democrats, much less Republicans. Legislation was in the hands of just a few Democrats, including John Goldmark, the chairman of the Ways and Means Committee. Goldmark was something of an oddity. He was a Harvard lawyer who had settled in the conservative eastern Washington area called the Okanogan Valley. He was a very good politician and had proved almost unbeatable despite the fact that he was an advocate of social spending and high taxes that were out of step with his rural constituency.

Goldmark was the author of something called the Tax Equalization Bill. While it sounded good, it was really an effort by the Democrats to sneak a property tax increase past citizens. Liberal legislators wanted the additional tax money to spend on their favorite social causes. The new property tax was particularly hard on farmers, and Goldmark represented many farmers. Yet he was so personally popular that he was virtually undefeatable.

The Association of Washington Business decided one of its goals should be to defeat Goldmark. But it had no idea of how to do it. I suggested the tactic that I had learned from Democrat Bob Perry: a straightforward letter written citizen-to-citizen explaining the issue. The AWB turned the project over to me. I contacted a well-known farmer in the Okanogan Valley and asked to come up to see him. I sat down with him and explained the Tax Equalization Bill. It didn't take long for him to see that the bill would open the way to doubling taxes on farm land. The farmer said he would be happy to sign a letter attesting to this to his fellow Okanogan farmers.

Next I hired a woman to go through the Okanogan Valley primary voting records and look up the addresses of all voters. That produced thousands of addresses. Now I had to get them all addressed before election day (this was before computers). I had an assistant who was a good Catholic and who knew the sisters at the House of Good Shepherd, an organization that took in unmarried pregnant girls. It is true that I did make several contributions to the House of Good Shepherd, but the nuns thought it was just great anyway because the girls were learning something about citizenship. We stuffed the farmer's letters in the envelopes, put several mail bags full of them aboard my plane, and I flew them to the Okanogan Valley so they would have a local postmark. It wasn't a very complicated political strategy. It didn't take a genius to guess that people who were working hard on dirt farms would not take kindly to having their taxes doubled by their own representative. In the election Goldmark was soundly defeated.

That campaign had a long and bitter sequel. Ashley Holden, who had formerly been the conservative writer for the *Spokesman-Review* in Spokane, was the owner of a weekly newspaper in the Okanogan Valley. Holden was an absolute right-wing extremist and he had a distinct aversion for all liberal people that would be hard to explain in today's society. In editorials in his Okanogan Valley newspaper, Holden accused Goldmark of every kind of sin, including treason. Goldmark sued for libel. In his libel suit he included all those who had participated in the campaign against him, including Luke G. Williams and the Okanogan Valley farmer who had signed the campaign letter. Goldmark had extended his objections to what

Ashley Holden had written to any and all who had contributed to his defeat.

In the ensuing court case, Goldmark's lawyer depicted me as a right-wing extremist and part of a plot. He presented the campaign letter and described to the jury how I had delivered thousands of them to the post office. I volunteered to take the stand and simply admitted everything, including getting the farmer to sign the letter. I explained, though, I didn't do it as part of a right-wing plot, but because there was nothing I could have done that was more beneficial to Washington business than defeating John Goldmark. Many people saw Goldmark's lawsuit as an effort to intimidate past and future political opponents. Kinsey Robinson, the chairman of the Washington Water Power Company and a conservative Democrat, donated money to our defense on the grounds that it wasn't conservatives but business that was being threatened by Goldmark's intimidation. We lost the case, but a short time later a higher court elsewhere in the country ruled the opposite on a similar case and set a precedent that rendered our verdict null and void.

Business was fighting an uphill battle in the 1960s. Not only was the state legislature in the hands of Democrats, but it was in the hands of the most liberal wing of the state Democratic Party. The Association of Washington Business tried to represent the importance of free enterprise to create jobs, but it was difficult to do when the machinery of state government was in the hands of liberals. The Speaker of the House was John O'Brien, a liberal Democrat from Seattle. I considered him a union stooge, which did not endear him to me. Under O'Brien, the Democrats were pouring on taxes in order to pay for programs that would get them elected. There was nothing the business side of the legislature could do about it, because the Democrats had a sizable majority in the House and John O'Brien ran the show.

At an AWB meeting I proposed the idea of working with conservative Democrats to elect a less antibusiness coalition Speaker of the House. The speaker was elected by the whole House. I reasoned that if we could rally all Republicans for a particular Democrat, and if he then brought along some Democratic votes of his own, he would be a speaker in a less partisan legislature. We decided that Representative Bill Day, a chiropractor and a moderate Democrat from eastern Washington, would be a good choice. It happened that I was a patient of Day's and so I agreed to talk to him. I always suspected that Bill Day was really in politics because he was a chiropractor and at that time insurance companies would not pay chiropractors for their services. His number-one mission was to get a bill passed that would allow chiropractors to be paid through insurance like other medical practitioners. Day agreed to buck the top leadership of his own party and run for speaker. He drew a good deal of Democratic support and solid Republican support and won.

Needless to say, he caused a heck of a lot of gnashing of teeth on the part of Democrats, not to mention the displaced speaker John O'Brien. Nevertheless, it saved the Washington business community untold headaches and untold millions of dollars in taxes.

A few years later we found that the same problem had developed in the state Senate: Democrats were in the majority and that majority was in the control of the most liberal faction. Senate leader Bob Grieve was the all-powerful signal caller, and quite hostile to business. Again we managed to form a coalition of Republicans and more conservative Democrats to take over the leadership of the state Senate. Doing so caused a horrendous fight. Grieve erupted on the floor of the Senate and announced he was going to expose the personal sins of all those who had

In the early 1970s I took the staff of the Association of Washington Business on a fishing trip to Mexico as a reward for their great work while I was president of the organization. I'm at the far left, and Dave Gordon is next to me. Dave is my good friend to this day.

turned against him. Senator Bob Twigg of Spokane stood up and taunted Grieve to carry out his threat by all means. Grieve slunk away and it was the end of the liberal domination of the state legislature.

These battles changed the course of Washington state politics. John Bagnariol was elected Speaker of the House and Augie Mardesich was elected Majority Leader of the Senate. They were good, pro-business legislators who understood the importance of a solid business climate in the state. The pattern had been for Democrats to take over leadership of the legislature, and then for ultraliberals to take over the Democrats. After these battles waged by the Association of Washington Business, the general state government became gradually more moderate. It became impossible for one person or a small group of people to set the tone for the whole legislature.

In these battles the Association of Washington Business was brilliantly led by Dave Gordon. He was a fine family man who had a wonderful wife named Betty. Dave used to tell me how some day he was going to retire to Washington's San Juan Islands, one of the most beautiful places in the world, and write a book. As I write this, Dave and Betty are retired in the San Juans. In my last Christmas card to Dave, I asked him what his book was going to be about. He responded mysteriously that it was about the moon and the angle of an island in the San Juans. Anyway, it was his dream and I hope he will fulfill it.

About this time I decided I had been working pretty hard myself and needed a rest. So I dropped everything and flew off into one of the best adventures of my life.

11

Flight of Eagle II, or My Midlife Crisis

I had begun to fly my own airplane as a business convenience, but I soon became addicted to the freedom it provides. You can be almost anywhere within a few hours. One of my favorite trips was to fly to Mexico to fish at the beautiful Hotel Cabo San Lucas. I loved the fishing, the climate, and the culture.

Somewhere along the line I had developed this dream — or perhaps it was a midlife crisis. I wanted to get away from business and politics for at least a month and tour Mexico and Central America by airplane and motorcycle. It is not very easy to get away for so long when you are president of a company that is growing like mad. But we had some very good managers running things at the time and I was determined to get away.

The second problem was that I needed a partner for this adventure, but few of my friends were in a position to take so much time off. I asked American Sign's general counsel, Horton Herman, and he surprised me by saying yes. Aside from being our general counsel, Horton was one of Spokane's most prominent lawyers and a trustee of the Comstock Foundation, an important charitable trust in Spokane. He was very enthusiastic, but I thought when he explained the plan to his wife, Mazie, the answer would be otherwise. But Mazie said yes.

The trip I envisioned would be rigorous, at least for two middle-aged executives. I figured Horton was up to it, since he had marched through Africa and Italy with General Patton. Horton's greatest recommendation, though, was that he was a very good friend of mine and superb company.

I owned a Navajo twin-engine Piper, very air-worthy and very forgiving, which is one of the reasons I bought it. We loaded this plane with everything we needed and a lot we didn't need: an ice box, spare parts for the motorcycles, spare oil for the airplane, three suitcases, two Honda Trail "suitcase" motorcycles with 90 horsepower engines, four fishing rods and gear, $120 worth of fruit and other groceries, some booze, three small suitcases, two large army duffel bags chock-full, a four-man rubber life raft, two sleeping bags, two cots, considerable camera gear, including three tripods and 90 rolls of film, maps, three briefcases, clothes, a spare tire, and a three-gallon thermos jug.

The only way we could get everything on the plane was for one of us to pull the last items in the door and then crawl or wriggle through this accumulation to the cockpit. Because of the weight distribution, the motorcycles went on first, which meant that every time we needed transportation everything had to come off the airplane. Whenever we went through unloading all of this at an airstrip, the local natives would get considerable entertainment from seeing all of this come out of the plane. It was like the circus act where 20 clowns emerge from a Volkswagon. Early in the trip, in Mazatlan, Mexico, we sent most of the excess gear home. It not only made the trip much more comfortable, but it probably allowed us to continue as planned.

We lifted off from Spokane's Felts Field on a cold, clear morning at 9:10 a.m., October 29, 1971. We flew to Casa Grande, Arizona the first day, where we happened to come across several members of the Hecla Mining Company board of directors who happened to be there on an inspection trip. Horton was a member of this board. We had dinner with them that evening and the next morning we lifted off at 10:45 and headed for Nogales, Mexico.

One of our first real ambitions for the trip was to fish the famous Mulege River, a river on the Baja Peninsula that empties into the Gulf of Mexico. The Mulege's outlet into the Gulf of Mexico is right at the Serenidad Hotel. The setting is tropical, with palm trees and banana trees along the banks. Early the next morning we walked the 100 yards from our room to the dock, where a boat and guide were waiting. I caught a seven-pound corvina and a smaller grouper. When Horton caught a corvina on a fly, he fulfilled a life ambition and proclaimed the trip already a complete success.

That afternoon we rode the Hondas up to Mulege to take some 8-mm movies. We visited a cathedral and the Baja Territory Prison, which held only seven prisoners. They were allowed to roam the little town at will because there evidently was no way to get far from Mulege without transportation. The prisoners

Horton and I pose with "The Eagle" with the two motorcycles we carried aboard it.

were allowed to hold day jobs, and each night reported back to their cells. As we roared from place to place, trying out our motorcycles, two boys ages 12 and 13 ran behind us, catching up each time we stopped, just to see the motorcycles. We let them get aboard and gave them rides, which they thoroughly enjoyed.

We were three days into the trip and having an absolute ball. Each night or while flying I dictated the events of the day and an entry at this point signals our settling into our freedom: "Luke's mustache is beginning to show." A second entry showed we still had a way to go: "Horton's bike broke down and after getting it back to the hotel and putting it through several overhaul procedures, we found out that the primary problem was that it was out of gas."

One of Horton's excuses for taking six weeks away from a very prosperous law practice to bum around Central America was that he was going to become fluent in Spanish. An entertaining aspect of the trip turned out to be Horton's word duels with postmasters, taxi drivers, and other locals. I entered in my log: "His enunciation is really good and he does real well insofar as understanding what people are saying and he can communicate with them also. In any event, he is showing promise of being an accomplished linguist, that is in Spanish, by the time we get back to Spokane."

In Oaxaca de Juarez, Mexico, we visited the 2500-year-old ruin, Monte Alban, and a nearby native market. Open-air vendors sold goats, turkeys, chickens, pigs, and just about any other type of animal. The food on display included beef, dried and otherwise, sausages, and bakery goods. The bread was delicious. I was intrigued by the pharmacy, where lines of baskets full of leaves, twigs, and plants offered native cures for rheumatism, asthma, heart problems, diarrhea, and just about any other malady known to man. As if that were not indication enough of the lack of local medial care, we saw many people who did not look healthy at all. Many people suffered from glaucoma and the number of blind people struck me. Across the street from this busy market the children of the vendors played in a great churchyard. Horton and I managed a conversation with five or six boys on the steps of the cathedral. They were delightful kids, but the contrast between their lives and the lives of typical U.S. boys was sobering.

We headed for Guatemala City. As we started down for a landing, the right engine began vibrating and shaking and I thought we might lose it. We weren't in any trouble because we were already at a low altitude when the engine began acting up. We were worried, though, about where we were going to get any service for a Navajo airplane in Guatemala City. We talked to the base operator and he quickly connected us with a mechanic who took care of seven Navajos. He adjusted the fuel injection system (which I had had completely overhauled in Spokane) and it was working fine by the time we took off.

The thing that we noticed was how hard people seemed to work. The hillsides were terraced into fields and each field seemed to be as perfectly tended as a garden. I recognized corn and it was amazingly tall — I estimated 10 to 14 feet by the way it towered over the shacks. All of the agricultural work was done by hand. Along the road we saw many Indians walking from work. Some of the women could not have been more than three and a half feet tall. Men were not more than five feet tall, yet they carried tremendous loads on their backs.

At the Mayan Inn, our bellman was Juan Moral. He was about four feet tall, two and a half feet wide, strong as a bull, and very, very pleasant. The Mayan Inn overwhelmed us. You enter a fantastically beautiful tropical courtyard, a maze of vegetation and foliage. Our room had a fireplace (since we were at 6,600 foot elevation), necessary at night and in the morning. We went to the bar that evening for a drink and ran into a man by the name of Jack Prescott, who it turned out had served in Horton's Army division in World War II. We retired at 11 p.m.

At 4 the next morning we woke up to the sound of cannon fire. The boy who came in a couple hours later to light a fire in the fireplace informed us that the booming sounds were not a revolution, as we had guessed, but the signals that a new tribe had arrived in the town for the tribal dances that would take place in the town square. The day before this space between St. Christopher Church and St. Thomas Church had been vacant.

*My new mustache a few
weeks into the trip.*

While we'd had breakfast, it had been transformed into a city of tents and poplin lean-tos bulging with trade goods of every description. This market at Chichen Itza was one of the most spectacular things in Guatamala. I couldn't believe the amount of goods that had appeared in this place overnight. It was like walking to this town square and finding three new department stores had popped into existence. All of this would be dismantled the next day, to be recreated every Thursday and Sunday throughout the marketing season.

We watched as some of the tribes entered the square. The chief of the tribe came first, men next, women and children following last. All were very formal and correct in their mannerisms, their arms held folded in front of them as they stepped to the beat of their drummer. They marched to the entrance of the church, knelt and prayed earnestly for a considerable amount of time, after which they rolled out the tribal cannon and shot fireworks, which in some cases were two and three stage rockets exploding in the air above. Later hundreds of Indians performed ritual dances in unbelievably intricate and beautiful costumes. This was pure native custom and not done for tourists. I have seldom seen such a spectacular show in my life.

The next day, Monday, we went to the airstrip to retrieve the Hondas and rode to Antigua, the former capital of Guatemala. We rode into the highlands, then down again into a valley. The beauty and splendor of the emerald and gray Guatemalan backdrop was breathtaking. I couldn't get enough of it. I will never forget the contrast between the dark clouds and the silver-white clouds and between the pale blue of the mountains and the vivid green of the vegetation. We stopped frequently to talk to natives, offering them a cigarette or cigar and asking them questions about the local area. They were invariably friendly, lacking any of the tenseness or harshness of people in a city in the United States or Europe.

We flew to San Salvador, El Salvador, on November 11. As we unloaded to retrieve the Hondas, the usual large and bemused crowd gathered to witness all the junk emerging from the small aircraft. We had become quite sensitive to this and decided to look for more things to ship home.

After breakfast the next morning, we started on the Hondas early, negotiated the traffic of San Salvador, and headed for a look at the volcano, Mount San Salvador. Immediately outside of the city was poverty unlike anything we had seen before. Children were playing around filth, papers, and squalor. Starving dogs barked at our heels. We saw one young girl methodically searching through a garbage heap for whatever of value she could find. Nevertheless, as we passed people pulling heavy ox carts or carrying huge loads on their backs, they smiled and said, "Buenos dias!"

The next day we had lunch at the Aero Club, the fancy flyer's club. We met Roberto and Ernesto Guiterrez, two young flight enthusiasts who cleaned the Hondas until they looked like new as a gesture of friendship. We insisted on taking them to lunch. They brought along a friend, Mr. Lopez, who left me with a lasting impression. He was about 24 or 25. He had been trained as a crop duster in Nevada and had been spraying for about four years. He had the carefree manner of a young devil as he described to us his several near crashes. He said from what he had observed among crop dusters the most dangerous time for pilots are the first and fourth years. He had the style of a World War I ace, and I reflected that crop-dusting in the mountainous country in those little airplanes had some of the same hazards as aerial warfare in biplanes. Horton and I agreed Roberto was one of the most delightful young people we had ever met.

After lunch I called the office, for the first time in two weeks. This was a record for Luke Williams.

That evening I recorded in the log: "It is about quarter to six and from the window in the hotel we can see the volcano, Mount San Salvador, and the sunset to the west is absolutely beautiful. Last night it was the most brilliant orange I have ever seen. Tonight it is a light yellow, but the movement of the clouds in this area make the change and contrast so apparent that it gives a definition to sunsets that I have not seen previously."

We lifted off from San Salvador at 10 the next morning and headed for San Jose, Costa Rica. Most of the distance between San Salvador and Nicaragua was over water. From 9,500 feet we could see both the Atlantic and the Pacific Oceans. We stayed at the Irazu Hotel and one afternoon we were walking through the lobby and heard absolutely beautiful piano music. We looked and saw an American man playing all by himself. The next evening at dinner we had a chance to meet this man, Ed Oliphant. It turned out he was a retired Navy pilot and had flown with the famous Navy Blue Angels acrobatic flying group. He had retired from the Navy and signed on to run a banana plantation for a group of friends. The plantation, about 75 miles north, had 3,000 acres of land and included 1,000 acres of banana trees, tended by 270 workers. He said the previous January it had rained 51 inches. His wife and four children had come to the plantation but after five months could take no more of the jungle and so returned to Key Biscayne, Florida. Ed said he was stuck where he was because he had built up considerable equity and had to see the investment through. He said he flew a helicopter down from the plantation to stay in the hotel to keep from going crazy. I believe that he felt he was really in something and couldn't get out very easily. He struck me as very lonely in his jungle paradise.

One thing Ed explained to us was why every native in Costa Rica carried a long machete knife in his belt. The area was home to three poisonous snakes, including the bushmaster that grows to eight feet long, five or six inches through, and had fangs as big as your index finger. Ed said a native could pull out a machete and cut a snake in half and never miss a stroke from his work.

We took off for Panama November 17, and on the way flew over a heavy cloud cover. I found a break and dropped down to 2,100 feet, but we entered a rain squall so dense it turned the cockpit dark. The control center asked if I wanted an instrument landing clearance, but I told them we were doing fine. I knew we had to break out very shortly because of weather reports. Such was the case and suddenly we were in full view of beautiful Panama City.

We spent a couple hours at a street market right in the center of Panama that is one of the most fascinating shopping spots I have ever seen. The whole length was splattered with sale signs and heaped with goods of every conceivable type. A cab driver took us for a tour of the ruins of old Panama City, once a haven for pirates.

Horton and I finally found a barbershop to get our hair and mustaches trimmed. An odd thing happened there. A woman who was waiting for her son to get a haircut noticed we were from the United States and said her husband's mother was from someplace called Spokane, Washington, and did we know where that was? Later the man whose mother was in Spokane, Jerry Andrews, called us and arranged to take us to dinner at the Pan-American Club. He was in business in Panama after getting out of the service there.

After two days in Panama we headed for Managua, Nicaragua. We were rather expecting a royal welcome in Managua. It happened that a friend in Spokane had gone to West Point and had roomed with Anastasio Samoza, the president of Nicaragua. Our friend, John Hayes, had written a letter to Samoza announcing our impending arrival, and we half expected to set down in Managua and be greeted by red carpets and its president. It really was rather funny because when we landed at the Mercedes Airport, there was not a single, solitary soul to be seen on the ground at the airport in Managua. When we got to the airport it was practically vacant.

Managua was one of the few places where I had a bit of business. The Banco Nicaraguense was considering buying a time-and-temperature sign and I had an appointment to talk to a vice president about it. He drove me out to one of their branches and showed me a new sign they had purchased, which had a Solari-type clock unit underneath it. It was kind of comical because the sign stuck clear out in the middle of the street, probably projecting about sixteen feet, which showed that they have the right kind of sign ordinances in Nicaragua.

That evening we had coffee and brandy at a sidewalk cafe in the downtown district. We were the only tourists there and a native guitar group was involved in a jam session which got wilder and louder as the players drank more and more. Everyone joined in the loud singing, punctuated with cowboy whoops and cheers. Viva Samoza Managua! They were really having a good time and some were drinking a little more than they should have, and it was really an interesting show.

We then went to Tegucigalpa, Honduras, where I talked to some more prospective sign clients. From there we wanted to visit the almost inaccessible Copan ruins of Honduras, which were usually open only to military and state aircraft. We got permission, but the weather was not good, with clouds at 1,500 feet. By the time we took off the clouds had thickened and lowered. Honduras is a very mountainous country and it is not any place to be fooling around in a broken cloud condition. I climbed to get above the clouds. The airplane was heavily loaded, and there is a limit to what even the Eagle II can do. At about 8,500 feet we got the first vibrations of a stall, but a flattening out of the nose provided instant therapy and we climbed out on top of a beautiful and vast field of silky white clouds in all of their splendor under a blazing sun. We spent about 20 minutes looking for the Copan Airport without success. We advised Cenemar Radio that we were not going to land at Copan and headed for Belize.

One of my aims in Belize was to purchase a wood-sculpted shark from the workshop of George Gullap for my secretary, Beverly Blick, and her husband, Clay. This took us on a long trek through the creamy mud and shambles left by the hurricane. Gullap is a wood sculptor of international fame. He had several students working in his shop and the work that we saw showed why he had such a reputation. These were in such demand that we had trouble buying one; all those on hand had already been promised. We got to meet George Gullap himself, who explained that all the sculpted fish were made by a nephew, Egbert Peyrefitte. We came away with the carved shark.

The next day we flew to Caye Chapel, a very beautiful small island about an hour and a half by airplane from Belize. We touched down about 5 p.m. and we thought it was rather strange that there were no airplanes at the airport. A man finally drove up to us. I asked if the hotel had any available rooms. He said, well, yes it did have available rooms, as a matter of fact, but there was one small problem, that being that the staff had all gone to Belize to escape the hurricane that had passed through the day before. This included the cooks. Suddenly all the food in the back of the airplane so many had laughed at was justified. Horton and I each had our choice of rooms in the hotel and we got a visit from the hotel's manager himself, a Welshman by the name of Don Stevens. The fishing guide, a New Jersey native by the name of Steve Burke, came to personally arrange our fishing trip. Steve was about 25 years old. He married a girl from Belize and seemed to be living in his own personal paradise. Scuba diving was his passion and he said the Great Barrier Reef at Belize was one of the finest places in the world for diving. There were shipwrecks all along it to be explored. About 30 miles away there was something called the Blue Hole, which was touted as being the greatest skin diving area in the world. He said it had stalagmites 140 feet under the surface that looked like something out of the Lost City of Atlantis. Jacques Cousteau had made movies there. (Much later, my wife Lucy spent a week on a live-aboard boat in Belize taking four to five dives a day. Her first night dive was on a 5600-foot dropoff near Lighthouse Reef.) Fishing the next two days, I reeled a barracuda to the boat, but we couldn't land him and he escaped in a swirl of pale blue ocean water.

When we returned to the hotel we found one more family had arrived, a Dr. Marco and family. He owned a small contact lens business in Miami. The family had four members and they owned four airplanes. Dr. Marco said they would regularly jump in an airplane without any planning and fly off for a vacation. They had flown all over Central and South America and as far north as Canada, Alaska, and Maine. We called them the Flying Marcos.

With no staff in the hotel, we cooked in our rooms for ourselves. We had done this before and so now got it down to quite an art. The total facilities were a single burner and one mess kit. Normal procedure was to take four drawers out of the chest of drawers and pile them upside down on the bed for a counter. You put the stove on the bureau, lit it up, and put all the hash and sausage in the pot. Since the pan heats very fast, it required a great deal of dexterity and nimbleness to see that everything came out at the same time and that the pan wasn't burned beyond reuse. The food was devoured with great enthusiasm, since it was all we had. Then the dishes were cleaned, the drawers put back in, the mess kit cleaned and reassembled, and then Alka Seltzer and Tums passed back and forth.

We flew on to the island of Cozumel (another diving mecca my wife Lucy has enjoyed). The airport there was totally abandoned. It was as if we had landed on the beach of an unoccupied island. We walked a mile or so up the road and suddenly came to a huge hotel looming out of the jungle. We were flabbergasted at the size and beauty of the Mayan Hotel.

The hotel was named for a nearby Mayan ruin called Chichen Itza, which later that day we toured. It was eerie to walk alone among the evidence for such a mysterious and amazing people — now vanished into nothing.

The next morning, when it was time to leave for the airport and our next stop, Merida, Mexico, we were stopped in the lobby of the hotel by a tropical rain deluge. Before long the rain let up somewhat and we decided to make a run for the airport. We loaded all of our gear into the cab and we rode the Hondas ahead. Just about the time we turned into the airport, Horton's Honda quit, and at the same time the heavens opened up in a torrent of rain the like of which I have never witnessed before or since. I made the mistake of telling Horton to hang on to the back of my bike, hoping I could tow him. He was reluctant, but I insisted it would work. Horton, not knowing that I am frequently wrong, but never in doubt, and with great bravery grabbed ahold of my cycle. I gave my cycle some gas and immediately Horton and his Honda went into a flat spin and ended up on the side of the road in an inch of water. He suffered a rather nasty abrasion on his elbow and his right knee and a sprain of some sort to his right ankle. We got his bike back upright, inspected it, and discovered that somehow his gas tank had been turned off, which explained why the motorcycle had quit. We rode on to the air terminal, loaded and fueled the plane in the downpour, and finally got away during a lull at two in the afternoon.

We landed at Merida. It is always quite a ceremony to land an airplane in a Mexican airport. There were no less than eight people out at the plane as soon as we were parked at the ramp. There was a policeman, a Customs officer, four or five gas people, two porters, a guard, and a couple of other people whose duties I did not know. There wasn't all that much traffic at these airports and when a plane came in, everyone wanted a part of it. We checked into the Pan-American Hotel about 5:30, put on ties and jackets and had a delicious dinner of abalone cocktail and fried chicken.

We awoke about seven in the morning and Horton seemed to be suffering a little from the wrenched knee. You would think that the poor dear was dying. Since it had been my idea for him to grab onto my motorcycle, I had to wait on him hand and foot, tie his shoes, pick up anything he dropped on the floor, some of which I think he did intentionally, all the while listening to Hortie explain what a dumb idea it was to have him grab onto my cycle. (I had begun to call him Hortie. He complained about this too and said it was evidence that the month we had spent together was too long.)

By about 10 o'clock I'd had all I could stand of this and took a walk. I hired a horse cart in the center of town and rode through the market area. I was very impressed with Merida. A friend in Mexico City told me this was the town where he wanted to retire, and I could see why. Merida was probably the nicest city we had seen on the whole trip. The climate was perfect that time of year and the streets, gardens, and homes in its prosperous neighborhoods magnificent. I have never seen a cleaner city. Everyone seemed busy and prosperous. I don't think I've ever been in a city where there seemed to be so many people with so little strain or uptightness. Everyone was pleasant.

We flew from Merida to Veracruz, Mexico, and then on to Mexico City. There I wrapped up the business portion of my Central American trip with Julio and Enrique Botello and Jorge Rivero, our business partners in Mexico City. We spent a couple of hours going over the requests for sketches and proposals in Central American banks. I still write an annual Christmas card to Julio Botello, a good friend. At this time he is 84 years old, works five days a week, and is still running a company with hundreds of employees.

We left Mexico City December 1 and headed for the small town of Guanajuato. Before departing Mexico City, we went through our supplies and distributed armloads of excess food to people who happened to be standing nearby. Before I could get out of the airplane again, about ten more women and children suddenly appeared around the plane to receive more. Where they came from I'll never know, since there was only about one house within sight of the airport. We were so close to our final destination that we gave all but bare essentials away. As we were nearing the end of the journey, we splurged and got a two-bedroom suite with a veranda and two sitting rooms.

A guide took us to the Castillia Santa Cecilli, an ancient mine mill that had been converted into a hotel. It contained all sorts of fascinating tools and machinery from the seventeenth and eighteenth centuries, when Spain ruled Mexico and extracted from it the precious metals that financed the Spanish empire. An ancient water drainage system had been converted into subterranean roads. In the era of Spanish rule, one of its mines, the Vellincia, at one time produced 75% of all the silver in circulation in the world. There were still fourteen active silver mines and they were the primary industry of the area.

The following morning our guide, whose name was Jesus, picked us up at 8 a.m. and took us to Kalores Hidalo, a beautiful old city with a magnificent church. It was Sunday morning and many people were out in the streets in their best clothes, going to church or to visit relatives and friends. The plaza was filled with nicely-dressed people and the weather was delightful. This was a farm community largely unchanged by the twentieth century and it was a fascinating glimpse of old Mexico. After we returned to the hotel I hired a 14-year-old guide to show me the city on the Honda and we drove around on the Honda for about two hours.

As we packed that evening, it was the first time we had actually spoken about going home. We had made it an unspoken rule not to talk about the day the trip would come to an end. All good things have to come to an end sometime.

We flew over the U.S. border the next morning and bucked strong head winds to Las Vegas, where we landed just to gas up. We soon took off again and looked for Reno as night began to fall. I believe Horten was maintaining a rather puckered position for about the last hundred miles. He kept looking over the nose of the airplane, as if he could steer me around obstacles, and asking me if I was sure that we were above the mountains. By the time we got to Reno it was pitch-dark. The air was clear and the neon lights of Reno glittered against the dark landscape, a beautiful sight.

We checked into a hotel, dined, and were, as was our custom by this time, asleep early. The next morning Hortie wanted to sleep in but I told him I could almost smell the pine trees of Spokane. He bailed out of the sack and we were packed and in the air within two hours. We flew over familiar sights, Pendleton, Walla Walla, and finally Spokane.

We had been gone six weeks to the day. We had flown a little more than 60 hours, which translated into about 12,000 air miles. We had ridden our Hondas more than 500 miles over the rough roads of seven Central American countries. The combination of the Navajo aircraft and the Hondas showed us these countries from high above and up close, a wonderful way to travel.

The flight of the Eagle II was a fulfillment of a dream I had had for a long time. The final entry in my log of the trip said, "I sincerely hope that, time and The Lord permitting, there will be other flights of the Eagle II in the future." There were many more flights. By one mode or another I traveled to every part of the world, from China to the Middle East. But there was never another trip quite like this one.

The approach control in Spokane must have wondered what I was doing, taking a very wide downwind approach to Felts Field. Horton and I were having a close look at home before landing. I didn't know it then, but the city I was looking down upon that day, with its railroad yards strung out along its riverbanks, was about to undergo drastic changes. The effort to bring this about would occupy much of my time for the next five years.

12

Expo '74

When I ran for the city council in 1962 the downtown business community was seeking federal funds for a drastic re-configuration of Spokane's Central Business District. Like many cities, Spokane was suffering from the drift of commercial activity to the suburbs. Major businesses downtown wanted to consolidate and upgrade the Central Business District so it could maintain its importance as the hub of the region's trade. The plan was to use federal Urban Renewal funds to build a local government complex at the east edge of Spokane's downtown to limit the spread and dilution of business. More federal funds would be solicited to develop a park and cultural center along Spokane's Riverbanks to stop the spread of the shopping district in that direction. This plan, the so-called EBASCO Plan, failed because Spokane voters voted overwhelmingly against it.

I was glad these plans were rejected. I did not believe government enterprise was the solution to business problems. In my judgment government would do nothing but inhibit private interests from pursuing the normal development of the city. When I went onto the Spokane City Council at the end of 1962, Spokane had a Department of Urban Renewal of 45 people. One of the first motions I made was to close this department. The council must have agreed, because my motion passed unanimously. I can still remember the reaction, though, from others. Good friends who had congratulated me on being elected to the city council would not speak to me. They would walk across the street if they saw me coming. Many people had convinced themselves that if only the government got involved, Spokane's problems would automatically be solved. I felt that all government involvement did was to hamper private enterprise. I think proof of the pudding was that immediately after we closed the Department of Urban Renewal, Spokane entered the biggest period of development in its history.

Government was better organized to regulate business than to enhance it. An example was the long battle over the development of NorthTown, a shopping center on Spokane's north side. Certain downtown business leaders did everything they could to prevent the opening of a shopping center in the 1950s. Dr. David Cowen, a dentist and the owner of a large downtown dental office, was chairman of the city's planning commission. As long as he was chairman there just wasn't going to be a NorthTown. Fortunately, Earl McCarthy, founder of NorthTown, was an aggressive competitor. He finally got the shopping center built.

For the same reasons, I had reservations about a proposed "Skywalk" system, walkways that linked Spokane stores at the second-story level. Most of the buildings linked by Skywalks belonged to the Cowles, Spokane's most prominent family, and a few other major property owners. Taking the traffic of shoppers to the second story and narrowing it to a relatively small part of town hurt of lot of small independent businesses down at the sidewalk level and beyond the core area. I had no problem with downtown businesses pursuing their own economic interests. The Cowles and other big property owners had a responsibility to protect their investment in downtown Spokane. If they didn't, it would soon look like the East Bronx, New York. The problem comes when you enlist government controls and incentives, which may benefit some but not all. They needed to depend upon their own initiative and their own risk to bolster their property values.

When downtown business leaders failed to gain Urban Renewal funds and to prevent the spread of business to NorthTown, they had to get more creative. The organization of downtown businesses called Spokane Unlimited hired a man by the name of King Cole, a planner and a very capable person from San Leandro, California. Cole proposed the idea of renewing Spokane's Central Business District by holding a World's Fair. This seemed very far-fetched when he proposed it. I have to give credit to those who could see the possibilities in Cole's proposal, most prominently the Cowles family, President Kinsey Robinson of the Washington Water Power Company, and Rod Lindsay of Lincoln Savings and Loan Association. They and a few others had the courage to invest in a private initiative with far-reaching consequences.

This was in the early 1970s and the American Sign & Indicator Company was running like a well-oiled engine. We had 600 or 700 employees and a reputation in the community as an example of the kind of business the community needed. I was on Lincoln Savings and Loan's board, and Rod Lindsay asked me to join the executive committee of Expo '74.

Much to many people's surprise, King Cole came back from Paris with the certification Spokane needed to host the World's Fair. The next problem was getting the cooperation of the state of Washington, since it had to be the political sponsor of the undertaking. I worked on this effort. My lobbying efforts on behalf of business in the state had given me a lot of contacts in the legislature. I was not particularly close to Washington's Republican governor, Dan Evans. Though both in the same party in the same state, Dan Evans and I had never been politically compatible and we both knew it. Evans, who was serving his third term as governor, had been elected for the first time in 1964, the year Barry Goldwater was running for president. Since I was promoting Goldwater and the Republican ticket both, Evans and I spent a good deal of time on the campaign trail together. But Evans was a liberal Republican. During the whole campaign I never once heard Dan Evans say anything good about Barry Goldwater, his party's candidate for president. Given the fact that Evans was elected and Goldwater was not, this might have been smart politically, but it always bothered me. Nevertheless, Governor Evans appointed me to chair the Washington State Commission for Expo '74. I'm sure he did so because I was on the Expo board, was a prominent Republican, and could work well with both parties in the legislature. I have always appreciated the fact that Governor Evans overlooked our differences and gave me this prestigious appointment.

There were a lot of skeptics about Spokane's ability to pull off a World's Fair. Though I was not among the skeptics, I was not an enthusiastic believer, either. I agreed to serve on the Expo board strictly because Rod Lindsay was chairman of the Spokane local Expo '74 committee and he asked me to do it. One benefit of rebuilding our city through our own efforts was that it required cooperation. For a small city to put on a World's Fair was a tall order. Most people in Spokane realized this and decided to set aside their personal concerns and rivalries and join the overall community effort.

One exception to this general rule that has always bothered me was the refusal of the Spokane Expo Board to accept one of Spokane's most distinguished citizens, Walter Toly, as a member. Walt was president of Columbia Lighting Company, which was one of Spokane's oldest and most successful companies. I knew Walt well and he was probably the best salesman Spokane ever sired, a fact he proved when he was put in charge of selling exhibition space for the Fair. For some reason, Bill Hyde, employee of the Cowles Publishing Company, did not approve of Toly. Hyde represented a major source of money that was going into Expo and he personally was able to block Toly's membership on the board. I always thought this was a great injustice and a great loss to Spokane's exposition. Walt was given the job of finding businesses wanting to display and advertise their products at Expo '74. One of the prospects was the Ford Motor Company. Lee Iacocca was the head of the Ford Motor Company at this time. A great deal of the fanfare and promotion for the Fair was based on the beauty of the Spokane River and the wonderful waterfall that ran right through the Expo '74 site. The Ford Motor Company decided to send a contingent of people out to make the minimal decision on whether they wanted to sponsor a pavilion or not. Their trip was scheduled for the middle of August, a time when there is barely a trickle of water going down the Spokane River and the waterfall is virtually nonexistent. Walter arranged lunch for the Ford contingent at a restaurant overlooking the falls. When they arrived the Spokane River was spectacular, flowing like the spring run-off. It looked absolutely stunning on that hot summer day. The Ford Motor people were very impressed and subsequently signed up to sponsor a pavilion. Prior to the meeting Walter had convinced Kinsey Robinson, Chairman of Washington Water Power, to open the dam near Coeur d'Alene, Idaho just for the occasion.

By 3 p.m. following the meeting, the river was almost dry again. Later, during Expo '74, I had lunch with Lee Iacocca and told him about what Walter did; he had a great laugh, because like Walter, Iacocca was a great salesman. This is an example of how the business community of Spokane pitched in to make Expo '74 happen.

Another great contribution came from Jim Cowles. Jim succeeded in getting the railroad company to re-route their tracks off of Havermale Island to free the site for Expo '74. Arguing railroads out of their tracks was not easy. Without executive skills like this, there would not have been a World Expo in Spokane.

Rod Lindsay is another example of Spokane's finest rising to the occasion. Rod used his considerable political skills to keep the Expo committee on an even keel through many trying times. Peter Spurney was the executive manager of Expo '74. I have often said that King Cole invented the Fair, Peter Spurney ran it, and Rod Lindsay kept it together.

The plan of Expo was to put on a World's Fair that would permanently benefit the city by leaving behind useful improvements. Clearing Spokane's riverbanks would contain business development in the downtown area and create a permanent river-front park for Spokane's citizens. Our current Riverfront Park was paid for from the profits of Expo '74. Some exhibition buildings were built to have residual uses after the Fair. Spokane desperately needed a convention center to attract more tourist business. My assignment was to help convince the Washington State Legislature to construct a World's Fair exhibit building which would look and act like a convention center once the Fair was over. I did not expect this to be too difficult. A convention center would stir up economic activity, and economic activity in its cities was well within the duties of the state legislature. We managed to get the legislature to allocate $7 million to the state exhibit, which would eventually become Spokane's convention center.

But after the money was allocated, the original plan changed. We had over a hundred committee members on the Washington State Commission for Expo '74. Some of these people had very different ideas about what the state should build in Spokane. One day I rushed out of one meeting and arrived a little late to a planning meeting of the Commission. As I walked in, a woman connected to Spokane's symphony orchestra made a motion that the state build an exhibit that could be used later, not as a convention center, but as an opera house. The motion passed with very little discussion. Our plans for a convention center were derailed that quickly.

I felt it did not make much sense for Spokane to acquire an opera house when it was desperate for economic development. To keep the possibility of a convention center open, we changed the plan so that it would include buildings that would serve the purposes of both a convention center and an opera house. But that raised the price to around $10 million. Those who had lobbied for the initial $7 million, including King Cole and Rod Lindsay, had been told by legislative leaders, "Do not come back for more money under any circumstances." Both King Cole and Rod Lindsay told me they would not go back and ask for the additional $3 million. So I had to.

My task was doubly complicated by the fact that both houses of the legislature were under Democratic control. My best hope was to convince Martin Durkin, a prominent Democrat and chairman of the Senate Ways and Means Committee, of the sense in a plan that included an opera house *and* convention center. I drew in a breath and called him and explained the problem. We agreed to meet at Seattle's Olympic Hotel. At dinner one evening, I told Durkin candidly that an opera house would turn out to be a financial burden. The City of Spokane might not care to take over that burden after the Fair, and that would mean the state would have to do so. Attaching a convention center, on the other hand, would provide the money the city needed to support the opera house, and would stimulate Spokane's and the state's tax bases. Durkin listened sympathetically and asked me to come by his office in Olympia.

When I showed up at his office, Durkin picked up the phone and called the scheduler of the Senate Ways and Means Committee and said he wanted a hearing on the matter of the state's Expo exhibit — immediately. The next day I was the only person to appear before Durkin's committee. After I spoke, the committee followed Durkin's recommendation to pass, with just one dissenting vote, the additional $3 million allocation. As people shuffled out of the room, I was still close enough to hear Durkin's aide, Mike Lowry (a future governor of Washington), say, "Isn't that the son-of-a-bitch that was Goldwater's state chairman?" Durkin said, "Yes." "Then why are we helping him?" Lowry asked. Durkin didn't answer him. My guess is that I had convinced Durkin that the opera house the state was going to build would turn out to be a white elephant in the long run, and poor exhibit space in the short, unless it was connected to a money-generating convention center.

Ultimately the compromise produced the single most successful by-product of the World's Fair for Spokane. The Spokane Opera House, designed by local architects Walker and Reuel with floor-to-ceiling windows overlooking the Spokane River, provided the cultural focus of Spokane. The architects originally had planned for 1,500 seats in the Opera House. But Joe Rosefield, a member of the facilities committee, said that was too few seats to attract a Broadway show. So we decided

Opening night of the Spokane Opera House, May 1974.

*Bea and I dressed up
for the inauguration
of Spokane's new
Opera House.*

with Joe's recommendation to construct the Opera House with at least 2,500 seats for the three million dollars. Even with the extra money provided by the legislature, we came up short for finishing it. So I asked Vicki McNeil to chair a fund raising campaign for Opera House seating ending up with 2,700 seats. Vicki raised $900,000 by selling reserved season seats for $10,000 apiece. Now the Opera House was complete. Vicki was an absolutely wonderful citizen of Spokane and ten years later served as its mayor. The combined Opera House and convention center finally put Spokane into the major leagues for attracting conventions, and has been a contributor to the city's economy ever since.

The formal dedication of the Opera House and Convention Center at the opening of Expo '74. Spokane Mayor Rodgers is on the left, Gov. Daniel Evans, Expo Chairman Rod Lindsay, and me.

Expo '74 was a complete success and a turning point in Spokane's history. Spokane gained a 100-acre city center park, general downtown renovation, and a dramatic increase in new businesses. Expo was an example of what private enterprise could do to rebuild a city on its own initiative. There was considerable city, state, and federal investment in Expo. U.S. Senator Warren Magnuson, especially, went to bat for Spokane. As chairman of the Senate Commerce committee, he could do about anything he wanted, and he got $11 million for the United States pavilion for Expo. I appreciated his efforts so much that I donated to his next election campaign — the only time in my life I ever donated money to a Democrat's campaign. But if one were to compare what the state got for $10 million, a vibrant opera house and a moneymaking convention center, with what came of the federal government's $11 million, a perpetually money-draining facility, one would never need to have another example of the wisdom of having local intelligence involved in deciding how to allocate government funds. The important thing about Expo was that it was not a government program but a private initiative that drew many participants, including governments.

Bea and I had a great time during Expo '74. Bea was a wonderful first lady of the state's Expo commission and I can't recall anything she ever enjoyed more. She contributed to its social success, as we entertained dozens of dignitaries who came to Spokane that spring until October. We entertained most of the country's governors when they visited. We escorted President Richard Nixon and his wife Pat through Washington's exhibit of great American paintings. (The president was relaxed and seemed totally fascinated by the artwork. I noticed no worry or preoccupation in him, though he was then under great pressure because of Watergate and would in fact resign his office just three months later). I will never forget touring Bing Crosby, an old Spokane boy, and his wife Kathy through the Opera House. Bing stood at the center of the large stage and tested its acoustics by singing a few notes of his "Boo-boo-boo" in that famous voice. I mentioned to Bing that his old movie partner, Bob Hope, was scheduled to appear in Spokane, but at the city's Coliseum, not this Opera House. Bing kidded, "Hope can't appear in a place like this. This is for *artists*."

During the six months of the Fair Bea and I met people from all over the world. Among the people we got to know best were the managers of the Soviet Union exhibit. The USSR pavilion was the largest foreign exhibit, 55,000 square feet, all of it Soviet propaganda. One night Bea and I hosted a dinner for eleven Russian governors and the Soviet exhibit staff. The lavish, white-glove dinner, featuring silver basins of salmon, oysters, and all sorts of other American delicacies, was laid out in Spokane's finest restaurant in the rooftop room of the Ridpath Hotel. In my remarks, I welcomed the Russians to "a typical evening meal of an American working person." It brought down the house. The Russians had, if little else, great senses of humor.

Foreign exhibitors came from many countries including Australia, Canada, Germany, Iran, Korea, the Philippines and China. The Opera House hosted some of the most famous names in show business at the time, including John Denver, Marcel Marceau, Roger Williams, Ella Fitzgerald, Isaac Stern, Bill Cosby, Harry Belafonte, and Bob Hope.

Given my views on international politics, people are often surprised to learn that I became close friends with members of the Soviet delegation. But the people are not the government. In fact, of all the people in the world, Russians are the ones who remind me most of Americans. They are bold, brave, skeptical, and fun-loving. Boris Kokorev, Soviet Pavillion Director, and Igor Pervevsive, the political officer, and I became good friends.

Igor accepted an invitation to go fishing with me, and only as we were leaving in the airplane realized that I meant to fly to Montana. He became very nervous and said he was strictly forbidden by the U.S. State Department to go more than 25 miles from Spokane! I said going fishing in Montana was surely okay with the State Department. He insisted it wasn't. Finally I told him it was okay anyway because I didn't really want to go fishing but only to show him my favorite missile installation in western Montana. He was nervous until the moment he cast a fly-fishing line into the Clark Fork River in Montana.

Kokorev was a wonderful person but also a dedicated Communist. He would concede to me the U.S. had certain advantages over his country. But he pointed out that the Russian Revolution was only 60 years old. When the Russian Revolution was as old as the American Revolution, he would say, Russia would be better than America. He really believed it. Years later I was in a taxi-cab in London and the driver told me the traffic was backed up because of a big Russian space show in town. I asked the driver to take me to the headquarters of the show at once. I walked into the Russian exhibit headquarters, and just as I hoped, the director was Boris Kokorev. I sent my card in to him, and moments later Kokorev came bursting through the door full of warm greetings.

After Expo '74 was over, Spokane Mayor Dave Rodgers signed an agreement with Governor Dan Evans to buy the Opera House from the state of Washington on the same terms as Seattle had paid for its state-built Expo pavilion (now the Seattle Center) ten years earlier. I personally didn't think this was fair to Spokane. The state had gotten good publicity value out of its exhibit at Expo '74 and the five million tourists Spokane had attracted had paid state sales tax on everything they purchased. But the more practical problem was that the City of Spokane, after the expenses of the World's Fair and development of Riverfront Park, did not have the $2.5 million to buy it. When Mayor Rodgers asked Governor Evans if the state could donate the Opera House, the governor said emphatically no. The governor said publicly that he would use it to store wheat before he would give it to Spokane for nothing.

That was where the matter stood when Evans retired from office in 1976 and Dixie Lee Ray, a Democrat, was elected. I was determined to try again with the new governor. It happened that newly-elected governor Ray held a post-election Governor's Ball in Spokane. I, of course, could not go to a Democratic Governor's Ball, but I arranged a meeting with Governor Ray through Lois Stratton, a Democratic state senator from Spokane and a longtime friend of mine. I had served on the Spokane City Council with her husband, Al. Lois persuaded Governor Ray to take a tour of the state's Opera House the day after the ball, and I was waiting there to conduct the tour. After showing the governor the building, I turned to her and said frankly that I wanted to talk to her about ownership of the building. I told her the building was likely to become a financial burden to the state. I said Spokane was willing to take over that burden, but it had certain problems in doing so.

"What you are saying, Luke, is that you would like to have the Opera House but you don't have any money," Governor Ray said with a smile.

I said that was not exactly accurate. We did have some money. "How much?" the governor asked. I said, "About a dollar." She laughed and said, "I think I can get this for you." Governor Ray persuaded the legislature to donate the building to Spokane.

Expo '74 was a wonderful thing for Spokane. It changed the city culturally and physically. It brought activity that had been waning back to town. It brought dozens of new restaurants and stores. It created Spokane's magnificent Riverfront Park. It brought a great sense of pride to the community to know that Spokane could put on a world exposition and attract visitors from all parts of the world. It was a tribute to people like King Cole, who invented the Fair, to Rod Lindsay, who kept it going, and to investors like the Cowles family and Kinsey Robinson of Washington Water Power, who took the initial financial risks. Under their leadership, the city was completely renewed, and the miraculous thing is that the Fair made a profit. It was a tribute to the thousands of citizens in Spokane and throughout the state who pitched in selflessly to make it work and an example of what people can accomplish in a free society.

13

The Sale of AS&I and New Enterprises

The success of American Sign and Indicator after 25 years of business was phenomenal. Time-and-temperature (Double T) display became a standard identification device for financial institutions. By the late 1970s we owned $130 million in signs attached to banks and other businesses all over the world. Lease payments on the signs reliably poured money into the company every month. Less than one percent of the leases were not renewed.

The value of the Double-T was that so many people used it, relied on it, and counted on it. I hired a man by the name of Ray

Anderson to take surveys of the readership of the Double-T sign many times. In all of those surveys, there never was a time when readership of a time-and-temperature sign was less than 80% of the people who passed by. This is a phenomenal readership for a sign. Similar surveys had shown that the standard neon or plastic sign would get maybe 5 to 15%. Other media did no better. Only 15% of newspaper readers, for example, were likely to read a quarter-page newspaper ad.

The ultimate goal of all advertising is to build top-of-the-mind awareness ("TOMA," it's called in the advertising business), and surveys showed that as people looked up at the time or temperature, they registered and remembered the business behind it. The alternating time-and-temperature sign invented by me and my brother Chuck in 1951 turned out to command phenomenal public attention, and appreciation for the service at the same time. The sign became commonplace because it developed more top-of-the-mind awareness than any other affordable advertising media.

Yet there was never a time when the business did not face one crisis or another. There have always been people who don't understand the importance of signs to economic development (usually liberals) and they are constantly haranguing about "billboard blight." AS&I always faced the possibility that government might regulate the time-and-temperature sign into extinction.

The business was also based in an evolving technology and liable to be outflanked by innovations. When my brother Chuck and I first invented the alternating time-and-temperature display, there were no computers or electronic devices. The first Double-T mechanisms were contained in a box 3 1/2 feet high, 10 inches wide, and 10 feet long. It contained hundreds of relays to switch electric current on and off. With the advent of the diode to switch circuits, the control box was reduced to 12 inches square, and that would do much more than the big cabinet could do. It was with that technology that we built our first professional sports scoreboard in 1968. It had a cylinder several feet long that whirled and spun around at some ungodly speed.

To be innovative, we had to acquire technology constantly. This often meant acquiring the companies who were technological leaders. When electronics became indispensable, we bought the Electronics Products Manufacturing Company from Jim McGoldrick, a member of one of Spokane's oldest families and a vice chairman of Expo '74. We assigned operation of the company to my nephew, Bill Williams, Jr. Bill and his wife Judi Williams were both entrepreneurs of the first order. Much later they would go on to develop their own company, Telect, which in the 1990s employed more than 2,000 people in the Spokane area and grew to be a $300 million company.

The new Electronics Products division developed a line of products that built out from the basic idea of the Double-T. We bought a patent from Paddy Salam called Unisplay that was

very effective in posting flight information. We developed the product and used it first at the Chiang Kai-shek Airport in Taiwan. We became an agent for the Solari Udine Company, the world leader in train station information boards, and using that technology installed the train information system in Pennsylvania Station and Grand Central Station in New York City.

Bill Williams Jr. and wife Judi.

The electronics revolution that would expand the potential of the Double-T changing sign business was just beginning to open up. We built the first of the grand scoreboards now standard in all professional sports stadiums for the Cincinnati Reds in 1968. It was a major accomplishment for a small company. AS&I built similar signs for dozens of professional sports stadiums across the country, from Boston to San Diego, and Green Bay in between. We also built scoreboards for hundreds of university and college teams. By the 1980s, I doubt if many people in the country could go a week without seeing an American Sign & Indicator sign, when you consider the ubiquitous time-and-temperature displays, scoreboards, readerboards in airports, train stations, and other such places. In New York City, for example, American Sign and Indicator put up the programmable signs in Times Square, Penn Station, Grand Central Station, Madison Square Garden, and Yankee Stadium.

Around 1980, we received the $11 million contract to build the sign for the 1984 Olympics. Dozens of sign companies wanted the job. We got it because by then we were the premier electronic sign company in the world. Building that sign was a kind of Olympic event for a signbuilder. The electronics revolution was in full bloom and the sign would have to show off this state-of-the art technology. The sign we built became one of the talked-about aspects of the '84 Olympics. It instantaneously posted all results and kept viewers aware of overall standings. It had animation and video, new things on that scale at the time. It could not only post the winner and time in an event, but show the event taking place on a gigantic video screen.

I think I explained before that our business model was unusual in that we leased our signs rather than sold them. Since we leased signs, we were responsible day-in and day-out for the operation of every sign we built. This kept us on our mettle to design good signs and to keep an eye on them. On the other hand, this service guarantee was a difficult test for anyone who would claim to duplicate our business.

The single greatest crisis that faced AS&I arose from this decision to lease rather than sell our signs. Leasing meant we had to finance the signs and thus made AS&I heavily dependent upon credit. We understood this and provided for it in our financial plans. But when Jimmy Carter became president in 1976, he brought on the country a very serious state of hyperinflation. American Sign and Indicator had about $65

Chuck and I are in front of the giant signs we built for the 1984 Olympics in Los Angeles. When this picture was presented to me it was captioned, "Chuck and Luke Williams, Fathers of the Electronic Sign Industry." The Olympics signs were state-of-the-art and the crowning achievement of AS&I, which was by this time the biggest manufacturer of electronic signs in the world.

million in debt that was floating with the prime rate, and our interest went from 7 percent to 21 percent in less than two years. Our contracts needed to be amended to take into consideration such inflation. Other types of businesses were imposing cost-of-living increases, and I thought we were entitled to do so. Though lease contracts had already been signed, I reasoned that our customers would consider us a kind of partner in providing and maintaining signs that were a valuable asset to their business. The question was: how would we approach our clients with this request to increase their lease payments because of inflation we had not anticipated? This was a business problem of major proportions to AS&I. Our accountant, Ed Woodruff, among others in the company, agreed it was desirable, but that it was simply an impossible task. The cost-of-living increase was not in contracts customers had already signed, and if they didn't want to accept them there was nothing we could do to force them to do so.

I have always thought a good business executive is nothing more than a problem solver. You can have a great idea and a good plan, and both may work from the beginning. But even the most perfect business will be confronted with a constant succession of problems. Solving them one at a time is what keeps you in business.

I was pondering the potentially devastating problem of our debt burden when I went to Chicago on some other business. There I met up with Howard Moffitt, a salesman working out of our Los Angeles office. I did not know Howard that well. But as we had dinner one evening, I discovered he was an extraordinarily charming and sophisticated man. I learned later that he had been a gentleman's gentleman who had once tutored upper class British schoolboys. Howard turned the simple act of ordering wine at dinner that night into a little ceremony that

An AS&I Specta Color Sign in Times Square announcing the arrival of my two grandchildren.

AS&I salesman Jim Turner and I under the sign we had just built for the Cincinnati Reds professional baseball team.

at once showed his mastery of the subject at hand and endeared him to the wine steward. It occurred to me that anyone who could please a Chicago wine steward had unusual communication abilities. Then and there I broached the idea that Howard might transfer to our headquarters in Spokane and take over the task of seeking cost-of-living concessions from our customers. A little to my surprise, he accepted the difficult assignment.

The results were amazing. Most of our customers agreed to pay the cost-of-living increase without complaint. The change netted American Sign and Indicator Corporation about 4 to 4 1/2 percent of our entire lease portfolio of $130 million each year. Howard Moffitt proved to be one of the best personnel assignments I ever made. He was a delightful person and he and I became great friends in Spokane. I was devastated by his sudden death in 1980.

It was in 1981 that I had a call from a security broker in Seattle saying that a man by the name of Bill Tuxedo, president of the Brae Company of San Francisco, wanted to see me. Tuxedo, about 45, pleasant and well-dressed, appeared in my office and announced he wanted to buy AS&I. I assured him AS&I was not for sale. But I consented to listen because I was curious about his assessment of AS&I and what made it interesting to him. I had not talked to Tuxedo very long before I realized he knew a lot about the leasing business, more than anyone I had ever met outside our own company. He assured me that, based upon his experience in the leasing business, American Sign was a very valuable property.

I was impressed enough that I accepted his invitation to go to San Francisco and learn about the Brae Company. There I learned that the Brae Company leased railroad cars to railroads. They had a method of tracking freight cars as these traveled all over the United States and changed from one rail company to another that was quite impressive.

When I came back I reported what I had seen to Chuck and Don Sherwood, my only two partners in AS&I, and said that we should expect an offer from Brae. I was adamantly against considering their offer. But Chuck was in debt due to bad investments in a recreational development in the Spokane Valley. Don was getting older and had been considering wrapping up his interests and retiring. They said they might be interested in selling if the right offer came along. We talked about our business and came to the conclusion that it was probably worth around $8-10 million, $12 million tops.

Tuxedo came to Spokane again, this time bringing with him Larry Hershfield, a bright MBA who had studied our company carefully. In a meeting at the Red Lion Hotel in the Spokane Valley, Hershfield made a very detailed presentation about our company and ended by saying he figured AS&I was worth $20 million. Would we sell for that? Chuck, Don, and I kept straight faces as we said we would think about it.

This price was much more than we ever expected. I still did not want to part with the company that had been my life for three decades. The trouble was, any way one figured it, this was too good an offer to pass up. So we told Tuxedo he had a deal. I decided, however, to retain 15% of the company and accept Tuxedo's invitation to stay on as president. I was only 58 and I loved the company and wanted to continue to work there. Don Sherwood advised me against it. He thought staying involved with a company others were buying for their own uses was bound to lead to complications. Once again, our longtime advisor Don Sherwood was right, but I didn't take his advice.

We couldn't figure out how the Brae Company was going to make money after buying the company for so much. But I got a hint. Not long after Tuxedo's first visit, I was giving him a tour of the AS&I plant and I mentioned that I was concerned about the amount of debt the company had, but that I had heard of a company that resolved this problem by selling leases to outside investors. Tuxedo didn't change his expression when I said this, but that turned out to be what he had in mind in buying AS&I. The Brae Company formed a private limited partnership in which they sold units in the AS&I lease portfolio to investors. Merrill Lynch Brokerage Company sold the limited partnership shares.

But it didn't work out as Tuxedo had planned, for the limited partnership went bankrupt. I don't know what went wrong with Tuxedo's program, but I always suspected he did not take proper account of the performance clause in our leases — the same thing that gave bankers pause when we began in the early 1950s. We stood behind our signs. (This was quite literally true. More than once Chuck and I had removed our ties, pulled on coveralls, and got up behind a sign to figure out why it wasn't working.) Only that kind of guarantee kept customers happy with a machine that had to work perfectly every minute, twenty-four hours a day. We figured out how to live with this demand, but the bottom line was that the performance clause limited the value of the leases to 36 hours — the amount of time we had under the contract to get a malfunctioning sign working again. Selling the leases as if they were free and clear of the maintenance obligation really wouldn't work. It may have been that those in Tuxedo's limited partnership figured this out somewhere along the line and decided they did not have a totally secure lease portfolio.

To get around my reluctance to sell, Tuxedo had insisted he wanted me to stay on to "mentor" the company. Then just before he sold the AS&I leases, he unceremoniously fired me and demanded I vacate my office immediately. They had managed to transfer all of the value of AS&I into the lease portfolio. I was not involved in the sale of the lease portfolio in any way. As I was a shareholder in AS&I, this transaction cost me about $3 million. I would have been that much ahead if I had taken my friend Don Sherwood's advice and cashed out of the company at the time of the sale. I have little doubt that Tuxedo eventually figured out that he had paid too much for the company. I suspect they were mad about it and happy to find a way to get back at me. I hired a San Francisco law firm to represent my claim on the company. I recall that one month's billing from the firm was $54,000, which was terrible. But the firm got a judge to order Brae to pay me $2.3 million.

This was my share of the company Chuck and I had built up since 1946. Most of this, about $2 million, went directly into an effort to bail Chuck out of his bad investment in his Spokane Valley recreation venture. He had rounded up some other investors, but they would not invest in Chuck's Holiday Hills Resort unless we did, too. My part was $2 million, and it was all eventually lost. Chuck's idea of building a resort area on Liberty Lake was a good one, but he was twenty or thirty years ahead of his time.

I was not out of business for very long. I had a friend in Spokane, a fellow Rotarian, by the name of Norm Bishop, who had moved to Boise, Idaho. He called me from there and asked if I would loan him $500,000 to get in the telephone business. He explained he wanted to bring a new technology that helped telephone companies keep track of long distance phone calling times and bill for them. This was used in Boise and elsewhere but was not yet available in Spokane. I knew Norm was a wonderful salesman and I had confidence in his ability to carry out his idea, so I sent him the $500,000. But after he had made the basic investments, his wife refused to leave her home in Boise and move to Spokane! So Norm turned Northwest Telco over to me and wished me good luck. Suddenly I was in the telephone business. I had to start from scratch building up a management team (which eventually included my daughter Brenda, who was living in Boise at the time and helped with the operations there). I ended up investing about $3 million in the Northwest Telco before it turned a profit, but then it began making about $100,000 a month. One day Paul Redmond, CEO of the Washington Water Power Company, a giant electrical utility headquartered in Spokane, walked into my office and announced that he wanted to buy Northwest Telco. I realized immediately that it would be tough to compete with a company the size of Washington Water Power if it was going to be in the telephone business. When Redmond offered me $6.5 million for my company I thought I had died and gone to heaven. So just as quickly as I got into it, I was out of the telephone business, $3 million richer.

Clarence Monaco, whom I had known since high school, owned a company that manufactured and sold fire alarm systems to military bases. He got into a financial bind and asked me to invest about $400,000. I declined to accept Clarence's offer but accepted one from his son, Gene. I financed him and bought the inventory from the bankruptcy court and went into business with Gene. Later I sold my interest in the company for $1.4 million.

While I was involved with Monaco, I had begun looking for some diversification. Monaco had only one product and one customer. A man by the name of Paddy Salam contacted me about an invention he had made. It was a mechanism that opened flaps to form letters and numerals. They were reflectorized to show up with a very small light source. This was cheaper to manufacture and operate than the lighted bulbs on the face of a Double-T. I thought it was a great idea and was ready to buy the right to build it. I showed Salam's patent to two patent attorneys to get their opinion. Both of them advised me that the patent underlying the idea had been previously registered in 1916. One said buying the patent would be like buying the patent for a shovel. Based on this advice, I declined to buy Salam's patent. Instead, I started another company, American Electronic Sign, in 1988 to develop and manufacture a similar product. Ken Cummings, our engineering manager, and his team turned the Diamond Bright sign into an excellent product, probably the best highway sign in the world.

Salam sued me for patent infringement. I was so confident in our ability to show the patent did not belong to him that I refused to settle. What I did not know was that the judge in the case had a reputation for settling cases out of court, and this refusal made him mad. Then we found out the jury that would hear this very technical patent argument was made up of six women, none of whom had education beyond high school. The opposition's attorney showed up one day with an assistant, a young woman. Before he launched his case, the opposition attorney took time to explain to the all-woman jury that this was his young assistant's first courtroom experience, so he hoped they would excuse any nervousness on her part. You could just see the empathy pouring out as all of the women jurors smiled toward the new assistant. I began to realize I was in a heap of trouble. We lost the case and the judge ordered me to pay Salam $3 million for the idea behind the product we had developed. Taking the case to court cost me an additional $1 million. In return, though, American Electronic Signs had a clear right to manufacture the product, Diamond Bright signs. I think it was the innovative use of its reflector product on the Diamond Bright sign that caught the attention of the giant 3M Company, which bought American Electronic Sign from me in November of 2000.

It was the fourth business that I had developed and then sold for millions. Just before selling out my last business in the year 2000, I turned 77. I had a lot of stress from these last businesses and it may have contributed to a decline in my overall well-being. Upon reflection, I realize that I really did work too long and probably should have retired sooner from the day-to-day stresses of running a company.

14

Chairman of the National Association of Manufacturers

Among chief executives of major businesses the large amount of time and attention I gave to politics was fairly unusual. I don't think there's any doubt it traced back to my experience with the Andrews for Governor campaign in 1960 and the fact that I was so handily beaten by the last-minute negative campaign sponsored by labor organizations. I really believe that you have to get the hell beat out of you a few times in order to become really motivated in politics. I have always felt that if I had not been beaten so badly by the unions and the Democratic Party in the Andrews campaign, and Christensen's defeat, I would never have given so much time to political battles.

My work with the Association of Washington Business, a statewide business lobby, from the mid-1960s to the mid-1970s had given me a reputation for being astute politically. At the beginning of that period leaders of the Washington State Legislature tended to be liberal Democrats. By encouraging alliances among moderates in both parties, AWB helped to promote a more balanced leadership and business got a better hearing before the legislature.

It was about 1970 that the National Association of Manufacturers (NAM) decided to broaden their influence by connecting with state organizations such as the Association of Washington Business. As part of this tie, NAM was looking for directors from state organizations. Dave Gordon, AWB president, nominated me, and I joined the NAM board of directors in 1970.

When I arrived at my first NAM meeting I stood in awe of the giants of industry around me, such as the chief executives of Maytag, General Electric, General Motors, AT&T, and 3M Company. The National Association of Manufacturers is the oldest trade organization in the United States. It was founded in 1896 to represent the American way of business on the political front. One of its early accomplishments was to found the United States Chamber of Commerce. (By the way, another Spokane native, Eric Johnston, served as president of the U.S. Chamber for many years and later was an advisor to several U.S. presidents. The Spokane company he founded, Columbia Electric, became a major supplier to American Sign and Indicator. The existence of this excellent producer of electrical supplies was one of the reasons we could keep a national company like AS&I operating from a small city like Spokane.) The National Association of Manufacturers was then and still is the lead spokesman for manufacturing businesses in political matters. It represents virtually every business of any size in the country and no U.S. president or other political figure proposes economic matters without taking into account the opinion of NAM.

Most NAM board members were people who had climbed to the top of their industries without much practical involvement in politics. I am sure it was my practical experience with elections and lobbying, and the fact that I was never reluctant to step forward as a spokesman for free enterprise, that soon got me assigned to the NAM Executive Committee.

I was at home in Spokane one day when Jim Bienz, the chairman of the Armstrong Rubber Company, and John Fisher, chairman of the Ball Corporation, telephoned me on a conference call. They told me they and other members of the board felt it would be valuable to find the next chairman of the NAM board in the Western states. I replied that a chairman from the Western states made good sense to me and I would send them a list of possible candidates right away. Jim Bienz said, "Luke, we are not asking you to think about someone else. We want *you* to become chairman." I could not believe the largest industrial trade organization of the greatest industrial country in the world was asking me, an ex-sign hanger, to lead it. I instantly accepted. Bea and Brenda had both been listening as I had this conversation. As soon as I hung up, Brenda said, very appropriately, "Dad, you didn't even ask Mom before you accepted!" It was true. I literally accepted without hesitation. But I knew Bea would not object. I think that it was testimony to the love and respect that Bea and I had for each other that it never occurred to me that she would not want exactly what I wanted. I assured Brenda that her mom would be one of the greatest first ladies that NAM ever had and it turned out to be that way. Bea had a wonderful personality and she got along great with the staff of NAM. She was and still is loved by the people who knew her in that organization.

The NAM chairmanship was a five-year commitment: the first year Vice-Chairman, second year Chairman, third year Chairman of the Executive Committee, fourth year Chairman of the Finance Committee, and fifth year Past Chairman. I was the Chairman in 1982, while Ronald Reagan was president.

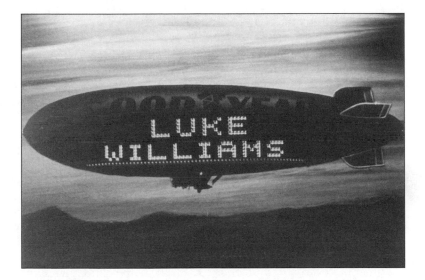

On the evening when I was installed as chairman of the National Association of Manufacturers, the chairman of the Goodyear Company came over to me and suggested we step out on the patio for a breath of fresh air. I looked up to see this.

The mission of NAM is to enhance the competitiveness of manufacturers by shaping a legislative and regulatory environment conducive to U.S. economic growth in a global economy. It tries to increase understanding among policy-makers, the media, and the general public about the importance of manufacturing to America's economic strength and standard of living. The most important issue in 1982 was inflation. During President Carter's term in office, interest rates soared from 7% to 21%. Fortunately he was followed in office by President Reagan, who had a thing about taxes. I don't think anyone in the country was more prepared to help the American economy than Ronald Reagan. It could not have been better timing for me to be chairman of NAM because I had known Reagan for years and we were friends.

The power of NAM was in the reputations of the well-known chief executives who made American industry work. I always deeply appreciated those who found time in their incredibly busy schedules to tend to the political work necessary to push such issues. Among the most devoted were Bert Lair, Chairman of the 3M Company, Stan Pace, Chairman of the TRW Company (who would follow me into the presidency of NAM), and Jack Welch, chairman of General Electric Company. These men and many others really understood the importance of legislation and regulation to the American economy. Consequently, they didn't send representatives to work with NAM. They did the work themselves.

Jack Welch was the most driven executive I ever met. He was like a General Electric clock—always precise and always working. I once sat next to his wife at dinner and I asked her what it was like being married to Jack. She said it meant being at work 24 hours a day. She told me that at seven every morning a driver and a secretary arrived at their door in a limousine. Jack got into the car and started dictating letters as he rode to his office in New York City. Late that night when the car pulled up to their home, Jack was still dictating letters and making phone calls.

A great fringe benefit of leading an organization like NAM is the chance to meet the titans of American industry. I remember being on the golf course with Herman Lay, owner of Lays Potato Chips, and I asked him how he got started in business. He said he had been running a small drive-in restaurant (I believe it was in North or South Carolina) and as a novelty he began slicing raw potatoes very thin and deep frying them, and lo and behold, the public liked them. He kept expanding his operation to keep up with the demand and eventually he built the Lays Potato Chip Company. During that golf game Herman told me he had eventually merged more than fifty companies. That very day, in fact, his company was set to announce that it had bought out Pizza Hut for $324 million. He asked me what I thought of it and of course I didn't know anything about the pizza business or the potato chip business. But I remember I won $6 from Herman Lay on the golf course and it was as if I had done something terrible to him.

I met Bill Boeing from my home state through the National Association of Manufacturers. His father, William Boeing, Sr., was of course one of the greatest entrepreneurs in American history. A German immigrant, he had made a fortune in timber and then went on to found Boeing Aircraft Company in Seattle and United Airlines. I never knew the senior Bill Boeing, since he died before I was involved in public matters, but his son Bill, Jr., understood the importance of public relations in business and worked at it tirelessly. I appreciated this because the importance of public affairs escapes many business executives, and yet it cannot be overstated. Regulations are one of the most costly things to the American economy.

One of the most fascinating people I ever met on NAM business was Armand Hammer, the famous oil magnate. Hammer was a phenomenally successful international entrepreneur with the peculiar specialty of dealing with communist and socialist leaders. I introduced Hammer as a speaker at a NAM luncheon, and we talked through the luncheon. He told me he had a Boeing 737 fitted out as an apartment and an office and he did much of his business in the stratosphere while flying from one place to another. I was struck by his personality and his obvious intelligence. It was one of the most memorable conversations I have ever had in my life. At one point he said, "Mr. Williams, Lenin told me . . ." and all of a sudden I recalled I was talking with a man who was once a confidant of the leader of the Russian Revolution! It seemed like I was sitting with a man from another epoch. Lenin died the year I was born, and here I was talking to one of his associates. Hammer was trying to convince me that the Soviet Union would have taken an entirely different course had Lenin not died so soon after the Russian Revolution. He said Lenin would never have nationalized all business in Russia the way Stalin had, and there never would have been the purges that cost millions of Soviet citizens their lives. I'm sure Dr. Hammer had no idea that there was not a person in the world who was more of an anti-communist than Luke Williams.

The most delightful — quite literally — person I got to know through NAM was Art Prine, the Director of Public Relations for the American Telephone and Telegraph Company. Art collected funny stories and told them expertly. On any occasion he could have an audience rolling in the aisles. He made a kind of science of cheering people up with humor. I told him I loved his stories and would like to have a few. He sent me a whole loose-leaf notebook full of them. My favorite was about the lady who went hunting for the first time. Her husband warned her not to let the California hunters claim her elk if she shot one. In the punch line she has her rifle trained on another hunter who is saying, "Okay, lady, it's your elk. But please just let me get my saddle off of it." I saw Art most recently in April of 1999, when he was giving out awards at a banquet. As usual, he had his audience roaring with laughter.

The best aspect of my NAM service was that it overlapped with the election of Ronald Reagan to the presidency of the United States. No president in my lifetime understood the importance of free enterprise and general freedom better than President Reagan. I had the honor of introducing President Reagan as a speaker a number of times. It was true that he was an actor, always reading his speeches from a TelePrompTer and performing them. I believe all great leaders must be actors. Franklin Roosevelt and Winston Churchill certainly were. With other members of the NAM board, I met with President Reagan and members of his cabinet. He was affable, laughing, pushing his jar of jelly beans down the table, but behind all that I knew he was certain of himself and what he intended to do.

I had first met Ronald Reagan almost twenty years earlier, in the early 1960s. Walter Knott of Knott's Berry Farms in California, whom I knew through the National Right-to-Work Committee, called me and told me they were trying to recruit the actor Ronald Reagan to run for governor of California, but Reagan was reluctant. Knott told me Reagan would be coming through Spokane on the train, and asked if I would meet with him and try to convince him that conservatives had a future in American politics. I knew Reagan only as a successful actor. At that time he was spokesman on television for the Twenty-Mule-

*With President Reagan. We had talked politics 20 years earlier at the
Spokane Club.*

Team Borax Company. Chuck and I met Reagan at the Spokane
train station and checked him in at the Spokane Club. That
evening we took him to dinner in the club's dining room. (He
told us that he had arrived by train because he did not like to fly.
Many times since I have reflected on this. After he entered
politics, he would spend much of the rest of his life on airplanes.)
During dinner we were constantly interrupted by people who
recognized him and came over to shake his hand. This was the
first time I had been around a real celebrity.

This first meeting with Reagan took place in the heyday of
Lyndon Johnson's Great Society. I tried to convince Mr. Reagan
that conservatives had a future in American politics. This was
the time to make a start, I argued, because Americans would
soon be tired of the Great Society. Reagan ate his dinner and let
Chuck and me do most of the talking. He didn't deny or refute.

He didn't agree. He just listened. I got the clear impression that whatever Ronald Reagan did about politics, he would make up his own mind and would not be persuaded by me or anyone else.

Later I read many accounts of people who dealt with President Reagan and I recognized the same trait. Soviet President Mikhail Gorbachev once complained that he couldn't persuade Reagan to change his opinion; it was Reagan's way or the highway. I really think Reagan was the type of person who ultimately relied upon his own counsel, and that was part of his greatness. He could not be talked out of anything he knew to be true. I am quite sure his convictions about communism came from his personal experiences dealing with communists in the Screen Actor's Guild in the 1950s. No persuasion by a charming Soviet president was going to change that. I believe it was Ronald Reagan's absolute understanding of the threat of communism that defeated it worldwide and brought freedom to so many people. I give prime credit for bringing about the collapse of the Soviet Union, the greatest threat to freedom and happiness in human history, to two men: Pope John Paul II, who successfully challenged it morally, and Ronald Reagan, who would not be talked out of his opposition to communist enslavement once he had made up his mind. In 1999, when Ronald Reagan was gravely ill with Alzheimer's disease, I wrote to his wife Nancy: "History will always remember him as the one individual whose dedication, understanding and perseverance really defeated the Communist empire throughout the world. It is one of the most significant episodes in the history of the world."

Ronald Reagan's presidency was a great satisfaction to me. Barry Goldwater had told me in 1964, when I was chairman of the Washington State Committee of Goldwater for President, that he expected to lose the presidential election, but that he had to make a credible run for it in order to keep the conservative spark alive for a later time. I believe conservatism and freedom from government domination and regulation finally obtained a great victory with the election of Ronald Reagan.

15

Bea's Death
and My
Remarriage
to Lucy

Bea really liked the Cruise-a-Home boat that AS&I owned. When we sold the company to Brae, I bought the boat at her suggestion and it was a source of great pleasure to both of us. We fixed it up and named it "B&L" for Bea and Luke. We had a lot of good times on it. We would cruise on Lake Coeur d' Alene, sit on the top deck, have a drink or two, and have great talks.

I believe it was about 1987 that I first noticed that Bea would talk about her childhood and her family repeatedly. I did not think much about it at first, but after a while I recognized that

Bea was starting to have a dementia problem. I knew that Bea's family had a history of Alzheimer's disease. Her mother and, I believe, two aunts had died from the disease on the Luuvass side of her family. It was about 1989 or 1990 that I had no doubts that Bea was going to be a victim of the disease as well.

Alzheimer's is a terrible disease. Everything that has ever been written about how bad it is is true, and worse. It is not a terminal disease, like cancer, but in a way it's more devastating. It simply destroys a person's mind and personality. First their memory goes, then their thinking capabilities, and eventually a perfectly wonderful human being can turn into a vegetable. It must be terrible for the victim until the disease takes away their ability to perceive what is going on in the world around them.

Bea and her sister, Rowena, who is about two years younger, were inseparable while growing up. When I met Bea, she and Rowena were sharing an apartment in the Roosevelt Apartments in Spokane. Bea was working for the federal government in the War Assets Division and Rowena was teaching at Riverside High School north of Spokane. They did everything together. I think they had coffee together every day of their adult lives.

Both Bea and Rowena were wonderful to their parents, Rudolph and Mildred Nordby. Rudolph was one of God's noblemen. He stayed on the farm until he was 84 years old and only the Lord knows what he went through taking care of Mildred while she was developing Alzheimer's. Bea and Rowena drove from Spokane to the farm in Genesee, Idaho, every weekend to help their parents through what must have been a terrible ordeal.

When Rudolph was 84 years old, he and Mildred moved to the Riverview Retirement Home. I am sure that the retirement home realized Mildred was in some stage of Alzheimer's and it did not take people who were incapable of taking care of themselves. But they made an exception for Mildred. Bea had been a trustee of the Riverview Retirement Home when it first opened and I'm sure it helped in getting Mildred accepted.

Mildred passed away in 1976. Rudolph, wonderful person that he was, lived a peaceful life at Riverview until he passed away in 1984. Bea and Rowena were the most faithful caregivers and daughters to Rudolph and Mildred and they loved them very much.

Bea's illness progressed slowly and steadily. Almost every month I would notice something that was not there before. Her entire life she would get her hair done weekly at the beauty parlor. Even after she began to show symptoms she drove herself so as to maintain as much independence as possible. Then after one appointment she took four and a half hours to find her way home. She got into a couple of minor accidents in the grocery parking lot, which resulted in cancellation of her car insurance. I had to take her keys away, but she didn't seem to feel too bad about it because she seemed to understand that she was no longer able to drive.

Thank God for television. It kept her occupied during the day. I had help come in every day so I could go to work. A couple of times while trying to cook, Bea nearly started a fire in the kitchen. I took over cooking our evening meal. Often we would go to the Studio K Restaurant. The waitress, Norma, was always especially kind to Bea.

Bea and I customarily spent three weeks of every year in Maui at the Aleua Village Resort. She loved it. Our routine was usually the same each day. Get up, have breakfast in the condo, take a walk along the wonderful beach. We would usually have lunch in the condo, take another walk, nap or watch TV, and go out to dinner.

As the Alzheimer's progressed, Bea did not do well with any change in routines. In 1994 I took her to Acapulco, Mexico, where we stayed at the Princess Hotel because it had a beautiful beach with nice bungalows. We had planned to stay for three weeks, but only stayed eight days. It was a strange place for Bea and she could not adjust to new surroundings. Coming home, we had to change planes in San Francisco and were looking at the television monitor for our gate to Spokane. Suddenly Bea just disappeared. She was gone and I almost panicked. I decided to stay put and in about five minutes she just returned. I realized then that she would require 24-hour supervision.

Being the primary caregiver for Bea was a huge responsibility for me and a source of constant worry, but I'm sure our bonding and love was strengthened during this time. My love for her was never stronger.

I took Bea to several doctors for help. Doctors who specialized in Alzheimer's were hard to find, and when I did find them they were even harder to get an appointment with. Still, we were able at least to get a definitive diagnosis and go on from there.

I had a friend, Dick Brown, whom we knew through the Manito Presbyterian Church. Dick's wife Aggie was two or three years more advanced with Alzheimer's than Bea. Dick became a great source of support to me. As Bea's condition worsened, I became less able to care for her at home, struggling to get her into the bathroom for showering and bathing. She contracted Parkinson's disease on top of the Alzheimer's, and as a result she was unable to stand or walk and became incontinent.

I was about at the end of my rope one day when Dick called me and said there was a room available at the same adult family home in the Spokane Valley where Aggie was. I went to meet Charlene and Wayne Henderson, operators of the home, and decided Bea would really be better off in their care. I talked to

Brenda, Mark, and Rowena, and they agreed. Bea moved into the facility in July of 1995. Brenda and her daughter, Bethany, decorated Bea's room at the Hendersons', taking great care to make it look like home.

We were all relieved and there's no question that Bea was much better off. But when I came back to the empty house that Bea and I had shared as husband and wife for over 45 years, the loneliness was profound. I walked over to the house of our good friends, Helen and Bob Shanewise, and just sobbed and sobbed.

I visited Bea almost every day at lunch or dinner time and fed her. She seemed delighted to see me each time until close to the end, when she barely spoke or recognized anyone.

A couple of months after Bea moved into the Hendersons', a blood clot broke loose and settled in her lower abdomen. She went to Holy Family Hospital, where a doctor told me that Bea could die at any time if the clot broke loose and traveled to her brain. So I was "prepared." Bea died on March 7, 1996, quietly and peacefully, while a caregiver was bathing her. Bea was a wonderful woman, wife, and mother of our two children. I loved her very much. We were married for 48 and a half years.

I was criticized, and probably justly so, for some indiscretions during Bea's long illness. As a matter of fact, I was traveling in China when Bea died. I regret that, but I make no apologies. There was absolutely nothing more I could do for Bea that would help her. I reasoned that she would not want me to stop living because of her condition, so I tried to live a normal life. No one can begin to pass judgment unless they have suffered the loss of a loved one in these circumstances.

I was 73 years old when Bea died and did not know what to do with the rest of my life. Luckily, I was still working five days a week, as chairman of American Electronic Sign Company, and staying somewhat involved in politics and the community.

In my wildest dreams I never thought that I would meet another woman to share my life with. But I did not know what the good Lord had in store for me.

When I was still caring for Bea at home, I tried to take her out for fresh air whenever possible. Bea loved to walk, but it became harder and harder for her as the Parkinson's set in. It was a sunny Sunday in May, 1995 when I decided to take her around a short block onto 33rd Street, the next street up from ours. Even though I chose a very short walk, Bea was struggling. I had her grasped around her waist, hoping not to let go for fear she would collapse. Finally her legs did give out and I struggled to hold her up. From nowhere, a woman came up behind us and grabbed Bea in the nick of time. Between the two of us we fireman-carried Bea back to our house. The woman who came to help was Lucy Bates. She had been watching from her front yard when she saw we were in trouble. She decided to leash up her dog and follow us in case I needed help. I thought Lucy was an angel who appeared just in time. It turned out that we were back fence neighbors. We had been neighbors for 17 years, but had never met!

Lucy had moved to Spokane in 1978 with her husband, Dr. Dan Bates, a prominent general surgeon, and two daughters, Jackie and Vickie. Lucy is a nurse with a master's degree in Public Health from the University of Michigan at Ann Arbor and experience in home health and hospice care. She had been assistant director of the Houston, Texas Visiting Nurse Association, supervisor for Detroit Visiting Nurse Association, and had worked in nursing in Portland and Spokane. In Spokane she had been a consultant and Clinical Director of Hospice of Spokane. At the time we met, her job involved traveling two weeks of every month throughout the United States surveying hospitals, home health care agencies, and hospices for the Joint

Commission on Health Care Accreditation. When I discovered she had all this expertise, I prevailed heavily upon Lucy to help me out with Bea, giving me advice on referrals and the appropriate level of care.

Bea died March 7, 1996. Hundreds of our family, friends, and business associates from a lifetime attended the funeral at Manito Presbyterian Church. Brenda gave a beautiful eulogy for her mother, as only a loving daughter could do. I was so proud of her.

Brenda, Mark, and other family members dispersed to their own homes after the funeral. The day after I was totally alone. There were a lot of flowers around I didn't know what to do with, so I called Lucy and asked if she would like some of them. I filled a vase with white roses and walked around the block to her house. I thanked her profusely for all her kindnesses and help with Bea. I cannot emphasize how much of a help she was to me in my hour of need. I asked Lucy if she would like to go for a walk, and we walked for two hours around the neighborhood. The next day, a Sunday, we decided to walk again, but in Riverfront Park and along the Centennial Trail in downtown Spokane. We talked and talked, about the funeral, about my feelings, about life, and I felt comfortable sharing anything with her. Lucy was in and out of town with her job. When she was in town we would sometimes have lunch. I could empathize with her rigorous travel schedule, as I had traveled extensively in my years of selling electronic signs to banks. Sometimes Lucy's husband Dan would join us on walks or for dinner. I met Lucy's daughters, who by now were away in college. I remembered glimpsing them many years earlier, when Jackie and Vickie were little and they would hop the wooden fence between our yards to chase their pet rabbits through our bushes, or when they were walking their large Newfoundland dogs in the park.

The next summer I asked Lucy if she would like to go for a picnic and boat ride on Lake Coeur d' Alene aboard my Cruise-a-Home. With a little help from Carlo Rossi wine, I plucked up the courage to kiss Lucy. I will never forget our first kiss — it changed our relationship, as we both knew we had become more than close friends. After the kiss on the boat, Lucy explained the importance of her Catholic faith and that she did not believe in adultery. I explained I felt the same way. With the passing of time our feelings grew stronger. We finally decided the best thing to do was for me to go over to the house and talk to Lucy's husband, Dan. It was early February, 1997. It took all the courage I could muster up to talk to Dan, not knowing if I would come home in one piece or not! I told him I was in love with his wife and wanted to marry her. Dan turned to Lucy and asked what she wanted. Lucy said she wanted to be with me. Then Dan said, "Well, I guess we better get a divorce." It was decided that Lucy would file the paperwork, and after 25 years of marriage, they were divorced. This came as quite a shock to Lucy's daughters, who were in college at the time. It was a surprise for my two grown children as well. But all of them seem to have adjusted over time.

Lucy and I were married August 1, 1997, at the Manito Presbyterian Church. Over 300 people attended the wedding and reception at the Spokane Club. Then we left on a six-week long honeymoon in Italy and Greece. My son Mark accompanied us on the Italian portion of the honeymoon. (Mark was one of Bea's favorite people in the world and we both love him very much.) Later Lucy and I witnessed our marriage in a small Catholic ceremony, on June 19, 1998. With two ceremonies, we are sure it will stick!

When we got home, Lucy crossed over the fence to move into the house Bea and I built in 1956. The wooden fence between the Williams and Bates homes has become rather symbolic. Jackie Bates was married in our backyard on Sept. 9, 2000. The bride, groom, and wedding guests arrived from the Bates home by stepping through the wooden fence slats. Jackie and husband Greg Hughes, who is from New Zealand, currently live with Dan Bates while Jackie completes her nursing degree (following in the footsteps of her mom) in Spokane. They visit by coming through the new gate in "The Fence." Vickie is still in college at the University of Utah.

Both Lucy and I keep busy with our involvement in Spokane community affairs. Lucy serves on three non-profit boards, and thoroughly enjoys the work. We also share the joy of exploring new places, of traveling to different countries with different cultures and customs. In our four years of marriage we have been to six of the seven continents. We have danced at the State Opera Ball in Vienna, in Washington, D.C., at the Inaugural Ball of President George W. Bush in January 2001, in Rockefeller Center's Rainbow Room, at the Fairmont Hotel in San Francisco, at luaus in Hawaii, the Caribbean and the Cook Islands, and at nightclubs in Singapore, Shanghai, Budapest, and Paris.

Due to the 25-year difference in our ages, Lucy is sometimes more adventurous than I am. I have enjoyed watching her whitewater rafting and jet boating in Queenstown, New Zealand, riding elephants in Thailand, swimming with dolphins in Moorea and Hawaii, petting wild manta rays and feeding sharks in Bora Bora. Lucy is a certified scuba diver — she would rather grow gills — but is content to snorkel so we can be together in the ocean (another first for me). Together we have viewed Iguazu Falls, Brazil from a helicopter and Victoria Falls in Africa. We have flown over Antarctica and sailed around the tip of South America in 70-mile-per-hour hurricane-force winds. We have cruised from Shanghai to Bangkok.

In my mid-seventies, Lucy introduced me to my very first major roller coaster rides. We spent a week in California with my son Mark, attending Six Flags, Knott's Berry Farm, Universal Studios, and Disneyland, screaming down every possible speed ride. I slid down my first water slide, at a speed of 63 miles per hour, at the Edmonton Mall, Canada.

In my wildest dreams I never thought my life would turn out this way, and that I would be doing such things in my golden years. We are both in our *first* childhoods and plan many adventures — as long as Lucy has the strength!

16

My Last Hurrah

O
n October 4, 2001, I turned 78 years old. I have a loving wife, Lucy, whom I cherish and love very much. My children Brenda and Mark and my two grandchildren are provided for. I have started a foundation for charitable purposes. I have made my peace with my Lord and Savior. I HAVE NEVER BEEN SO CONTENTED IN MY LIFE.

I have a neurological problem called hydrocephalus, a long word for water on the brain. My doctors have decided not to place a shunt to drain the fluid as there would be a high risk of intracranial bleeding. This condition is affecting my speech, the use of my fingers, my balance, and coordination. If it were not for Lucy's loving assistance with dressing, bathing, etc., I would undoubtedly have been in an assisted living facility long ago. Every time I begin to feel sorry for myself I think of Christopher Reeve, the actor who, at the height of his career, fell from a

Fishing in Alaska was good.

horse and became a quadriplegic. He has handled his much worse physical problem with inspiring courage. I also think about all the blessings in life the Lord has bestowed upon me.

Recently Lucy and I have begun building a beautiful home on Lake Pend Oreille in north Idaho. It is a thrill to see this longtime dream develop before us.

We have fondly shared a number of our travel experiences with Bob and Helen Shanewise, our good friends and fence neighbors. Lucy and I intend to travel more with them. As I write this, the four of us are about to leave on a safari to Botswana, Africa, and the Seychelles Islands.

Besides travel, there are certain things that are very important to me, including seeing those I love being truly happy. I also enjoy taking life by the horns and living it to the fullest. In other words, I intend to "Live" until I die.

I have worked hard throughout my life and some would say it is high time I just sat back and put my feet up. However, there are still a couple of things I would like to do. After all, having a purpose is what gives us all a zest for life.

I have started a new company called Trade Mark Advertising. I do not intend to get back into the manufacturing business again. Trade Mark will provide professional advice on how to utilize the electronic reader-boards. I am not in this for financial gain, but because I find it such a thrill to be involved with America's great system of free enterprise. There is something special about taking an idea and nurturing that idea into a real living and breathing enterprise.

The second thing I would like to do is to start the circulation of a public affairs newsletter called *The Public Affairs Bulletin Board*. With the vast array of communication technologies today, I believe there is a great opportunity to develop and pass on opinion. I feel such a forum is needed to help make people more politically aware. I once read that written communication played a key part in the foundation of early America. I have always had a great respect for the written word and have seen many examples of its power over the years, especially in the political arena.

One purpose of the periodical will be to explain the high cost of liberal politics to this nation. Freedom and free enterprise, I believe, are being eroded by liberals. Liberals prefer government enterprise to free enterprise. Because of this, I fear our great nation is being severely weakened and is on a fast track to European socialism. This is the last thing America needs and is definitely not the last thing I want to see happen in my lifetime. Liberals use taxpayer money to fund their liberal ideology. Liberals have given up the American Dream of "work hard and prosper." Having said this, both liberals and conservatives are motivated by the same thing, which is to have health and prosperity for their families. I cannot understand why some liberals are so antibusiness. To me there is nothing better than an American corporation which employs thousands of people around the world and contributes millions of dollars in revenue to the economy through taxes, payrolls, and charities. Liberals would have no government money to spend if it were not for American businesses and taxpayers.

Now that this memoir is done and about to be delivered to the printer, these projects should keep me busy.

As I said at the opening of this book, one of the reasons I wanted to write it is that I have had a wonderful life, and I give credit to the opportunities that were provided by our Founding Fathers in a system of free enterprise and individual freedom.

God Bless America.

Luke G. Williams
November 1, 2001
Spokane, Washington